D8191

Copyright: the Development and Exercise of the Performing Right

Performing Right

Gavin McFarlane

LL.M. (Sheffield), Ph.D. (London)
Barrister and Harmsworth Scholar of the Middle Temple.

ISBN 0 903931 27 3

CITY ARTS SERIES
General Editor: John Pick

John Offord (Publications) Ltd.,
P.O. Box 64, Eastbourne, East Sussex.

Printed by Eastbourne Printers Ltd.

For Stella, Neil
and Angus

A scribe; from a 12th century manuscript of Bede's Life of St. Cuthbert. British Museum, Add. MS. 39943 f.2

Preface

This book is largely the text of a doctoral thesis carried out at the London School of Economics, and eventually successfully presented to the University of London. It is intended to fill some gaps in the rather sparse writing on the subject of copyright, and to throw more light on the history of the performing right in this country. I have tried to show how that right has been exercised since its inception by the various interested parties, and in particular how its economic importance has increased with the rapid growth of the entertainment and allied industries. Copyright is a subject which is poised to spread in application far outside the fields of literature, music, art and drama which originally required its protection; with new legislation it may come to affect many areas of advanced technology, and will undoubtedly be of much greater significance in offices and the world of education.

I owe a good deal to the guiding supervision of Professor W. R. Cornish of the London School of Economics; he has already done much to advance the cause of copyright in the United Kingdom by his series of lectures, and his lively interest stirred me to research further areas which have contributed greatly to this work. Much assistance has at all times been willingly given by friends and colleagues during my own days in the entertainment industry, particularly those in the Performing Right Society. Mr. William Wallace CMG, formerly Assistant Comptroller-General of the Patent Office, gave me considerable help in tracking down records of early meetings and discussions; these would certainly not have been located without his aid.

Finally I must place on record the encouragement of my friendly publisher, whose unflagging enthusiasm is truly infectious. His active involvement in all stages of the preparation of this venture has done much to smooth my path, and I am delighted that my work should have been chosen to appear in his City Arts series.

G.McF.
Bassenthwaite Lake
Easter 1980

5

Illustrations

Contents

1
The Dawn of Copyright Protection

There are few references to the performing right in legal textbooks in this country. The matter has hardly been touched on so far in Britain as an academic subject. This is true of the whole field of copyright, though the general topic has been dealt with in textbooks of greater or lesser value from the early nineteenth century. From time to time, British writers who have achieved an international reputation have contributed to learned journals on some issue of authors' rights, but except for the specialised house magazine of the Performing Right Society, "Performing Right", these contributions have rarely been on performing rights as such. Now even "Performing Right" has ceased publication.

The situation is quite different on the continent of Europe and in America, where both copyright as a general study and the speciality of the performing right flourish, receiving encouragement both from the academic and commercial worlds. But unfortunately so far there has been little conscious discussion of the performing right here, or indeed much evidence that its existence as a separate right is appreciated. In view of the contribution which Britain has made to the protection of authors' rights over the centuries, this is disappointing.

In the **Copyright Act 1956,** the fountainhead from which almost all British copyright law at present derives, the performing right is dealt with at S.2(5)(c) as one of the six acts restricted by the copyright in a literary, dramatic or musical work. The restriction is simply against 'performing the work in public', and a similar restriction is embodied in S.12(5)(b) in respect of gramophone records against 'causing the recording to be heard in public'. There is however fierce opposition in some quarters to the treatment of this gramophone right as a true copyright, and the opposition will be examined in depth at a later stage of this thesis.

Now the performing right generates millions of pounds each year for the benefit of the right owners. Yet this is a comparatively recent phenomenon: the right only came into being here in any statutory form in the third decade of the nineteenth century, some forty years after its introduction in France. While the French right owners derived considerable benefit from it almost immediately, their British counterparts had to wait until 1914 and the formation of the Performing Right Society (PRS)

9

in this country before any worthwhile royalties began regularly to accrue to them. The question therefore poses itself. How did the performing right come to emerge from the general umbrella of copyright protection, and when once established, why did it take so long to bear fruit in the shape of worthwhile receipts for the owners of the rights?

Most historical accounts of copyright begin with a reference to the Statute of Anne 1709, because this is the first legislative instrument known anywhere to have established some form of protection in the nature of copyright as it is understood today. At this date it was well in advance of the Decrees of 1791 and 1793 which established the rights of performance and reproduction respectively in France.

In several countries where literary production and taste had advanced somewhat, less formal systems of protection had evolved based initially on licences and privileges, and in this country at least a certain degree of protection had sprung up in the common law, the boundaries of which were ill-defined. But the feeling that protection was needed seems to have evolved in a more recognisable form than mere grumbling at about the time of the invention of the first form of mechanical reproduction, that is the invention of printing. There had been complaints about plagiarism by authors from the dawn of literature, but it was printing and the commercial opportunities that went with it which first came to be defended.

It was the multipliers themselves who first called for protection, the early printers who felt the need for monopolies to guard their investment and its products against other printers. It was not the authors, but apparently the printers and bookbinders who exerted pressure to secure the passage of *25 Hen.c.15* (*Printers and Binders Act 1533*) which forbade the importation of books into the kingdom. Examination of the *Statute of Anne 1709* (*8 Anne c.19*) reveals that its preamble declared itself to be 'An Act for the encouragement of learning by vesting the 'copies' of printed books in the authors or purchasers of such copies during the times therein mentioned!' Clause 1 went on to grant to the author of a book already printed 'the sole right and liberty of printing such book for the term of twenty-one years' and to the author of any book not then printed a similar right for fourteen years. The right subsisted in printing and it was only through printing (or as we should now say, publishing) that it could be infringed.

This concentration on 'mechanical' reproduction continued in English law up to the *Copyright Act 1911* in which by S.1(2)(a), copyright included the sole right to produce and reproduce - nothing more. For the first time the reproduction protection was not specifically against printing. By the *Copyright Act 1814* (*54 Geo.3, c.156*), it had been the 'sole liberty of printing and reprinting' which was spoken of, and again in *S.2 Literary Copyright Act 1842* 'the word 'copyright' shall be construed to mean the sole and exclusive liberty of printing or otherwise multiplying'. It was apparently never contemplated by the draftsmen that anyone would go to the trouble of multiplying a work by hand. After the invention of printing certainly this would not have been a serious danger, but as we shall see, it had been a source of annoyance to writers before the coming of print.

So the early law gave more freedom to the copier than the present Act, for even manuscript reproduction is an infringement under the *Copyright Act 1956*, unless it is exempted in some way under the fair dealing provisions.

In an age when techniques of reproduction are becoming ever more sophisticated this is a curious anomaly. But even the *Lectures Copyright Act 1835*, which appears to be the first instrument to mention manuscript copying, merely contemplates the lecture being taken down in handwriting. The protection of the Act was aimed against subsequent unauthorised multiplication. Thus

' . . . if any person shall, by taking down the same in Short Hand or otherwise in Writing, or in any other way, obtain or make a Copy of such Lecture or Lectures, *and shall print or lithograph or otherwise copy and publish the same* . . . ' an offence under the Act was committed.

It is clear that in Britain at least any movements for protection in the nature of copyright have largely been motivated by the entrepreneurs of the artistic and literary world rather than by the creators themselves. As we have seen, publishers, printers and bookbinders were in the van of early pressure. Later, music publishers, and in the twentieth century record producers, film makers and broadcasting organisations have been energetic in lobbying for the protection of their interests.

But for many centuries, in fact for the greater part of man's existence, manuscript was the only known means of reproduction. During this time the mysteries of writing were known only to a tiny fraction of the populations of even civilised societies, an almost ritualistic art which nevertheless held the key to lucrative and dignified positions within the fabric of early states. No doubt force of arms and wealth controlled the destinies of empires and estates, but heads of kingdoms were generally illiterate throughout the Dark Ages, and indeed until comparatively recently. Even Charlemagne who stood out in those times as a supreme patron of the arts and learning only with painful difficulty learnt to read, but never was able to master writing, though by all accounts he tried hard enough.

Earlier, after the barbarians finally overthrew the Roman Empire in the West, the torch of learning was kept burning across the centuries in the bastions of Christian faith. These were the monasteries, which were long obliged to seek protection against the marauder and philistine in the remotest corners of the continent. Thus in Ireland, Iona and, legend has it, in pre-Viking Iceland, the studious monks copying by hand laboriously kept scholarship alive, and preserved knowledge for the next generation.

As men wrote, so other men arranged nevertheless for their productions to be multiplied in so far as the limitations of manuscript allowed. Such books were bound and put on the market, and research into these early times reveals that at every stage from writing the work to putting the bound copy on sale, there were interests which felt that protection was called for.

Dr. Marie-Claude Dock cites interesting details of book production in Rome in her work on the history of copyright[1]. Within the book trade the same group of entrepreneurs controlled both the production of books and the sale of them to the public, and they operated in their shops in the Forum and other places in the city. The original work written by the author was delivered to the bookseller, who had within his shop a department of copyists, generally Greek slaves, whose value in the market was quite high[2]. They took an oath to make exact copies, and were liable to punishment if they were found to have deviated from the original. The original was dictated in a loud voice and taken down by the copyists, who might number anything up to a hundred in a large room. Martial records that his second book composed of ninety-three epigrams in five hundred and forty verses could be reproduced in one hour by this method[3].

In the next room the process of collating and correcting the copies went forward, for often the texts contained numerous faults due to the speed of the dictation. Cicero records the complaints of writers[4]. Some conscientious book sellers employed qualified grammarians to correct the copied texts. Many were not so scrupulous, and their products went on the market full of errors, leading to complaints among the book-buying public in Rome and the provinces. The books were in rolls, not hinged, so there was at that time no need for bookbinders. The absence of the crafts of binding and printing may account for the slow development of a separate property in the literary work, as opposed to the manuscript which carried it.

---

1 Dock. Étude sur le Droit d'Auteur (1963) p.12,13.
2 Horace Ep.II,5.
3 Martial Ep.II,1,5.
4 Ad.Quint III,5.

Diverting accounts are given by Dr. Stephen Ladas of plagiarism in classical times[5]. He tells that Martial was probably the first to apply the term to literary property, for that writer had the habit of referring to his verses as his children. He called the thief of these 'children' a 'plagiarius', derived from the Roman law term of 'plagium' - the crime of stealing a human being[6]. Cicero also complained in similar terms that Epicurus "borrowed bodily all his physical theories, his philosophies as well, spoiled what he borrowed, and gave no credit at all"[7].

Dr. Dock traces the germ of the performing right in these early records of the literary world of Rome[8]. She claims that even the most bigoted opponents of the notion of a copyright in Rome admit the existence of a performing right then, and bases this assertion on the statements of two nineteenth century commentators. According to M. Caresme, playwrights 'in the middle ages as in Rome sold their works to local dignitaries, who put them on for the benefit of the public on festivals and holidays'[9]. M. Despois was more dogmatic; 'At Rome, the theatre was the only literary field where a living could be made without the support of patrons . . . copyright only existed in the theatre'[10]. Certainly Terence was known to have sold his plays, and as at least one of these sales was to an actor the subject of the sale was possibly the right to perform. Donat, in his commentary on Terence, says of *The Eunuch*, 'It was sold a second time, reproduced as though it was a new play'[11].

From this, Dr. Dock concludes that the first sale was only for the right to put the play on for a single performance, and that the subject of contracts between playwrights and theatrical producers in Roman days was a performing right of a kind and not the entire property of an unpublished manuscript. 'Without any doubt, there was the beginning of the recognition of a copyright, of a right independent of the property in the manuscript'[12].

.With respect to Dr. Dock, this is to draw too much from a single sentence in translation from the original Latin. It is the only instance cited by her of the practice, and may be no more than an example of the phenomenal success of the production allowing the author to make a

---

5 Ladas. International Protection of Literary and Artistic Property, p.13.
6 Martial's 'Epigrams to Fidentius' - Book 1, LIII, LXII, LXVI.
7 Snyder, 'The World Machine' p.134.
8 Dock. Étude sur le Droit d'Auteur,pp.30,34.
9 E. Caresme. De la propriété littéraire dans l'histoire et selon le droit. Nimes,(1864)p.6.
10 E. Despois. Revue des deux Mondes, (1859) p.781.
11 Publii Terentii Vita, II.
12 Dock. Étude sur le Droit d'Auteur, p.34.

1 *A manuscript illumination depicting a play of Terence being mimed by masked actors.*

second and possibly unauthorised sale of the manuscript. Certainly it does not justify the conclusion that there was a conscious performing right in Rome, which had the support of the law, while the nineteenth century authorities she cites are at best second-hand generalisations, giving no authority for the propositions put forward. The sale of plays is certainly referred to from time to time in classical literature, Juvenal speaks of the sale of a tragedy entitled 'The Agave' by Statius to the actor Paris[13]. But in the absence of any clear statement to the contrary, this must be taken to be the outright sale of the manuscript to an actor or producer, which was the usual practice for centuries. Ladas gives another example which seems nearer the truth of the practice[14]. 'And if therefore Titius has written a poem, a history or an oration, on your paper or parchment, you and not Titius are the owner of the written paper.' This was not the case with works of art. 'It seems to us the better opinion that the tablet should accede to the picture for it is ridiculous that a painting of Apelles or Parhadius should be but the accessory of a thoroughly worthless tablet'[15]. There was therefore no distinction being made between literary and artistic rights on the one hand, and on the other the property in the manuscript or tablet which carried the work. Indeed, prior to the invention of printing, a right against unauthorised performance would have been a more logical form of protection against exploitation than a protection against unauthorised reproduction.

When the curtain of barbarism fell across Europe, the demand for the books of the time must almost have vanished, and the only copyists practised their art in monkish cells. It was to rise again before the invention of printing, and the demand for copies multiplied in manuscript was renewed, but across these centuries the evidence of demand for protection is sparse indeed.

What appears to be a copyright suit of a kind is referred to in two separate sources[16] [17]. Although Roger Harben in his scholarly account of this dispute gives as his ultimate source Adamnan[18], the Irish saint and historian, who was ninth in succession to Columba as Abbot of Iona, it owes more to folk history than formal law reporting. But because there is such a dearth of evidence of copyright recognition for so many centuries, the details should be recorded here.

---

13 Juvenal. Sat.VIII, 87.
14 Ladas. International Protection of Literary and Artistic property, p.13.
15 Institutes, Book 2, Title 1, Sections 33 and 34.
16 Bowker on Copyright, p.9.
17 Harben, "Performing Right", April 1968, p.22.
18 Adamnan, Vita S. Columbae, (624-704).

As the legend has it, an action was brought in the year 561 A.D. against Saint Columba, the founder of the abbey of Iona. While he was visiting Abbot Finian, a former master, Columba took the opportunity to secrete himself by night in a church where the abbot's psalter lay, and copied it. Finian discovered this outrage by chance, and brought an action for delivery up of the finished copy made by Columba, on the ground that a copy made without permission should belong to the master of the original book. Columba declined to give up his infringing copy and the matter was referred to King Dermott in his palace at Tara. The King found for Abbot Finian and in the course of his judgement uttered this rustic phrase which has become an Irish proverb, 'To every cow her calf.'

History does not record whether the Abbot ever did obtain delivery of the document from Columba. As Bowker observes[19], the dispute indicates that even in those days there was a sense of copyright. Nevertheless the Abbot's psalter was not an original work in itself, but as an authorised reproduction it was felt to be entitled to protection. This may contradict more modern caselaw, which takes the view that a mere copyist of a written work does not obtain copyright in his copy[20]. It is thought however that copyright can be claimed in a work which is a piracy of another copyright work, though not if that piracy is a mere slavish copy[21].

Thus the copyright law which has developed since the introduction of printing might not have recognised Finian's rights if such law had existed at the time of the Abbot's dispute with Columba. Perhaps in those early times one's own authorised manuscript copy of a work could reasonably be regarded as requiring as much protection as an author's original work today. Probably what Finian was trying to protect was his right to control the use and accessibility of his book. It may be that his authority as Abbot rested on his possession of works which could be consulted to decide matters of policy, and to reinforce his control over his followers. No doubt Finian considered that for a subordinate monk in the same abbey to possess the same source of authority would strike at the basis of his own position. It is some justification for the bitterness with which the matter was fought out.

No other reference to a claim to a copyright or a performing right apart from Finian's is recorded between the close of the Roman empire in the West and the rebirth of intellectual life in Western Europe in the

---

19 Bowker on Copyright, p.9.
20 Walter v. Lane [1900] A.C. 539 at 554.
21 Copinger and Skone-James on Copyright, 11th edn., para. 145.

twelfth century. This "witnessed a renaissance of the European mind which, though more contracted in scope, is comparable in energy and creativeness with that great enlargement of customs and taste which divides the modern from the mediaeval world . . . the thirst for knowledge, which is one of the primal appetites of man, began to assert itself afresh . . . Guilds were formed of learners as at Bologna, of instructors as at Paris, and after the manner of their kind evolved a body of rules and regulations for their guidance"[22].

With this new upsurge in learning reference begins to be made to the manufacture of books in manuscript copies, and there are occasional references to privileges and guilds associated with these productions. These do not however lend much support to the view that there was an established performing right on the Continent of Europe in mediaeval times, still less in Britain.

Correspondence between Dr. Fell, the Bishop of Oxford, and the Archbishop of Canterbury[23] records that "multiplying and increasing books by writing was a privilege of the University of Oxford and all men and trades employed thereon were privileged persons of the University"[24]. The statutes of 1223 of the University of Paris provided that the booksellers of the university should produce duplicate texts of written works authorised for the use of the university and there is a suggestion that the university paid scholars for annotating and proofreading texts. At that time there was in France a guild of legalised booksellers (libraries jurés) under the regulation of the university. They exercised jurisdiction over the copying and censorship of manuscripts as a body of publishers and writers. In 1368, letters patent of Charles V specified fourteen "libraries" and eleven "ecrivains" as registered in Paris. They enjoyed the privileges of issuing certificates of the correctness of a manuscript copy, as well as the right to copy and sell in certain circumstances[25].

The germ of licences and monopolies undoubtedly existed in relation to manuscript work long before the invention of printing. According to Augustine Birrell "we are too apt to exaggerate the effect of mechanical contrivances"[26]. In his valuable and diverting collection of lectures on authors' rights, he expressed several times opinions of this sort. Thus "that there were books bought, books read and books collected before

22 Fisher. A History of Europe, p.245.
23 quoted in Gutch's "Collectanea Curiosa", Vol.I, p.273.
24 Briggs, International Copyright, p.27.
25 Bowker on Copyright, p.9.
26 Birrell, Seven Lectures on the Law and History of Copyright in Books, p.43.

the moveable types were invented is also certain"[27]. Again, "although the power of multiplication at work in the Dark Ages was below that which now exists, the difference was not so extreme as may have been supposed"[28].

These views are to some extent borne out by statistics. According to an important French writer of the early nineteenth century, there was evidence that there were 10,000 manuscript copyists in Paris and Orleans alone at the time of the invention of printing[29]. Gibbon queries this. "Before the invention of printing and paper, the labour and materials of writing could be purchased only by the rich; and it may reasonably be computed that the price of books was an hundredfold their present value . . . When Fust, or Faustus, sold at Paris his first printed Bibles the price of a parchment copy was reduced from 400 or 500 to 60, 50 and 40 crowns"[30].

Sir Arnold Plant, then Sir Ernest Cassel Professor of Commerce in the University of London, in his presidential address to the London Economic Club on 13 March 1934, also doubted the extent of manuscript production in the days before printing. He asserts that so far as is known there was never any thought of copyright in those times. Manuscripts were sold outright, the author knowing that the buyer might have copies made for sale; and the first buyer knew that every copy he sold was a potential source of additional competing copies. Moreover, copies of copies naturally fetched lower prices, for errors in transcription are cumulative; and the owners of original manuscripts could sell first hand copies at special prices[31].

The historian Fisher is still more dismissive of the extent of manuscript copying put forward by Dock and others. "The immense revolution in the intellectual opportunities of mankind which followed upon this last discovery (printing) may be inferred from the speed with which, in an age unhampered by patents, it spread throughout Europe . . . It has been calculated, but on an estimate which is probably too conservative, that by the close (of the fifteenth century) some nine million printed books must have been in existence as against a few score thousand manuscripts which, up to that time, had contained the inherited wisdom and poetry of the world"[32].

---

27 Birrell, op.cit., p.47.
28 Birrell, op.cit., p.45.
29 Augustin-Charles Renouard, Des Droits d'Auteurs (1838), p.25.
30 Gibbon, Decline and Fall of the Roman Empire, Vol.III, p.219, citing Mattaire, Annal, Typograph., i, 12.
31 Plant, The Economic Aspect of Copyright in Books, Economica May 1934,p.167.
32 H. A. L. Fisher, A History of Europe,p.465.

When in the twelfth century Europe emerged from the tunnel of darkness into the Middle Ages, literacy was virtually the preserve of the priesthood, which had long enjoyed a stranglehold on the offices of state in the majority of European countries. But all was soon to change. "Wandering students ranging from boys in their teens to grey-haired men might be seen on the roads travelling to such centres as were known to be distinguished by the presence of attractive teachers"[33]. As the art of reading swiftly became more widespread, so the need for copyright gradually became more urgent, until the invention of printing by Gutenberg in 1451 made the issue vital - at least in the eyes of the printers.

But before the advent of the printers and their demands for protection other crafts had been engaged even in manuscript book production, and it is likely that they also had pressed for protection for their activities. Prominent among these were the bookbinders, who subsequently joined with the printers in obtaining the *Printers and Binders Act 1533* which forbade the importation of books into England as a protectionist measure.

During mediaeval times the impracticability of the rolls used in ancient times became too inconvenient. The rectangular form with folded parchment pages sewn together in groups or sections came into existence, perhaps evolved in answer to a demand for greater permanence. These folded pages were enclosed in hinged boards covered with leather, and the new hinged form is substantially the hard-cover book of the present day. So the new trade of bookbinding came into being, for the old roll books had not required their services.

These new hinged books entered into use some time before the invention of typography. The laboriously copied manuscripts would be bound up in this way, often in another department of the same monastery which had produced the manuscript. But while clearly the copyist needed to be able to read and write, these qualities were not necessarily called for in the bookbinder. According to John Westwood, the binder did not even reckon to put the titles on the covers and spines[34].

Thus long before the advent of the printers the bookmakers and allied trades had established themselves as flourishing craftsmen practising a following with returns which were respectable enough, if not actually exciting. But with the invention of printing their life-style changed abruptly for several decades, for in their sphere a kind of technological

33 H. A. L. Fisher, op.cit., p.245.
34 J. Westwood, "Renaissance Bookbinding", Folio Magazine Jan. 1971.

2 *Forerunners of hard cover books in the chained library, Hereford Cathedral.*

revolution took place, as book production multiplied time and again. As the secrets of the new craft were taken across Europe by those versed in the skills of printing, so the production of books, or in other words publishing, became one of the first really international trades.

2
The Invention of Printing and the Early Cases on Performing Right

Gutenburg is credited with the invention of printing in Mainz in 1451, and Caxton introduced it to England in 1474, though there were suggestions that Corsellis had introduced it at Oxford in 1468 at the King's expense[1]. Inspired by the German printers and booksellers the "German Art" spread through Europe, reaching Italy in 1465, Paris in 1470, Stockholm in 1483 and Madrid in 1499. In 1494, only two years after the expulsion of the Moors from Grenada, three German printers were already established in that town[2].

The printers controlled bookselling, or publishing, at this stage, and though they did not actually control bookbinding, the fortunes of the latter were inextricably bound up with printing. At the outset there was a great demand for the products of the new invention, and increased book production led to increased bookbinding. Those with particular skills in the two crafts were able to move across frontiers with ease during the early boom years and follow their trades in foreign lands. At a very early date the statute *I Rich.IIIc.9 (Importation of Books by Aliens Act 1483)* allowed the free importation into England of printed books from abroad, and this liberty continued for about half a century.

There is a touching familiarity about the early history of printing, for, as with latter-day booms and technological revolutions, it was not long before overproduction of books led to a flooding of the market. Demand fell away, and those who had invested time and capital in speculation suffered burnt fingers. As early as 1472 bankruptcies were being recorded among printers in Rome, and a similar situation had reached Venice by about 1500. John Westwood records that among its other attempts to control the recession, the Stationers' Company tried by various means to discourage foreign bookbinders who had settled in England[3]. This might in part have been due to jealousy of the foreigners' superior workmanship.

---

1 Scrutton, The Law of Copyright, 4th edn., p.5.
2 H. A. L. Fisher, History of Europe,p.466.
3 Westwood, "Renaissance Bookbinding", Folio Magazine, Jan. 1971.

3   The earliest known depiction of a printing press, Paris 1507.

Enterprises of all kinds were subject to a system of royal patents, whereby needy monarchs gave themselves the right of granting monopolies and licences in many fields, in return for contributions to their exchequers. Printing was very rapidly brought under this control, not only for the revenue it would generate, but also because it set up a medium for persuasion and propaganda at least as striking in the fifteenth century as broadcasting was to become in the twentieth. Examples of the early profitable printing monopolies are: for all grammars in the Latin language; another for all Bibles; another for all dictionaries; and a fourth for all lawbooks[4].

In 1556 the original charter of the Stationers' Company was granted by William and Mary, when general control of the printing industry was entrusted to it, in an attempt to control printing on religious matters. Immediately a comprehensive attempt at rationalisation was made in the interests of its members. Wherever large profits had attracted interlopers, the case against uncontrolled competition was argued with great force by the Company[5].

Prior to the formation of the Stationers' Company, pressure from the English printers and binders had secured the passage of a piece of protectionist legislation in the shape of *25 Hen. VIII, c. 15. (The Printers and Binders Act 1533)*. This probited the importation of books, and at the same time offered some measure of protection to the public by fixing the price of home-printed books. The preamble to this statute observed that among the subjects of the realm were those who "have given themselves so diligently to learn and exercise the said craft of printing, that at this day there be within this realm a great number cunning and expert in the said science or craft of printing, as able to exercise the said craft in all points as any stranger in any other realm or country." As to the poor bookbinders they "having no other faculty wherewith to get their living, be destitute of work and likely to be undone, except some reformation herein be had." But in all this there was no mention of the author, the creator of the intellectual interest. What were being protected were purely commercial interests of capital and labour. In England at any rate at this time there was no sign of a reproduction right for the author, and still less a performing right for the dramatist or composer.

On the continent there are records that early privileges to print were granted to the author. These seem to have evolved from the continuation from manuscript days of certificates of approval testifying to the authen-

4 Plant, Economic Aspect of Copyright in Books, Economica, May 1934, p.175.
5 See in general Arber, A Transcript of the Registers of the Company of Stationers of London 1554-1640.(1875).

ticity or correctness of an edition. Bowker refers to such a certification by the Bishop of Ratisbon in relation to a tract of Peter Nigrus printed in 1475 in Esslingen[6]. Sabellico is known to have received one in Venice in 1486. As historian to the Republic of Venice he was granted the sole right to publish or to authorise the publication of his "Decade of Venetian Affairs" without the limitation of time, and a penalty of 500 ducats was prescribed for any infringement. In 1491 Peter of Ravenna, the author of "Phoenix" was granted the exclusive right to print and sell this work by the State of Venice. In Germany the first recorded privilege was issued by the Imperial Aulic Council in 1501 for the printing of the dramas of Hroswitha. As the author had then been dead for 600 years he was scarcely to be a beneficiary of the right!

One of the earliest examples of protection to an author, in the sense of creator, lies outside the field of literature. In 1512 the magistrates of Nuremburg confiscated certain counterfeit copies of engravings by Durer, on which the counterfeiter had forged the original artists' signature. This is without question a reproduction right, albeit in respect of an artistic work. The right even attained post-mortem extension, for the widow of Durer in 1528 obtained exclusive printing for her late husband's works from the authorities in Nuremberg, and still later in 1532 unauthorised re-engravings of his works were restrained by the Nuremberg magistrates[7].

So far as literary and dramatic works are concerned, there is no indication in the earliest days in England that there was a performing right for the author, and only limited privileges for the printers. What was the situation for music printing?

It seems fairly clear that the first book of music ever printed was a Gradual, of which the only copy still in existence is in the British Museum. It has neither date nor a printer's name, but the type used identifies it as coming from one of the presses operating in Southern Germany around 1473. This accuracy is due to the fact that the press which used this type had only a very short life, ending in that year or a little later[8]. The next work was a Missal printed in Rome, bearing the date of 12th October 1476[9]. These were the first printings of what may be called complete musical works, as opposed to the isolated use of single notes as illustrations to prose passages. Although the type-printing of liturgies spread quite rapidly through Europe it did not

6 Bowker, Copyright, p.10.
7 Bowker, op.cit.,p.10.
8 A. Hyatt King, Four Hundred Years of Music Printing, British Museum (1969)p.9.
9 A. Hyatt King, op.cit.,p.10.

appear in England until 10th January 1500 when Pynson printed a two coloured Sarum Missal. Around 1525 a new typographical principle was evolved whereby each note would be cast as a separate unit, with the adjacent portions of the stave attached to the stem and the head of the note. This was the beginning of a new era in music printing, for with various improvements it has stayed in use throughout Europe to this day, though latterly to a diminishing extent[10]

Towards the close of the sixteenth century the rise of the Italian aria and the birth of opera made the printing of music in score a necessity. Engraved prints therefore came into use at about that period, and thereafter first type-printing and then again engraving were to hold sway at different periods as the most popular manner of music reproduction, depending on what kind of music had the general favour at that time. New forces of musical and social change gathered strength as the centuries wore on, and new centres of production began to compete with the old. The introduction of chamber music and the replacement of the harpsichord by the pianoforte reflected the rise of a new middle-class hungry for music for domestic performance[11].

Gradually the printers and engravers developed their businesses, until some of them eventually became great music publishing houses. In Austria in the late eighteenth century a number of new firms sprang up, eager to profit from the Viennese school of composers led by Haydn, Mozart, and Beethoven[12]. But as with literary and dramatic works, there is no evidence of any performing right. Undoubtedly composers were paid, although perhaps often less than they would have liked. But the age of the orchestra and the concert was yet to come, and chamber music was designed more for domestic than public performance, so could scarcely serve as a spur to demand for a performing right.

In music publishing as in the book trade, new interests in property had come into being. Although at that time the rights were not specifically identified either by statute or general recognition the printers who controlled the trades knew that they required protection, even if they were not clearly aware that they had something intangible to protect. Agitation came from the printers and it was the printers who were accorded protection. Authors and composers sought no protection, and they received none, until agitation was made on their behalf much

---

10 A. Hyatt King op.cit.,p.15.
11 A. Hyatt King op.cit.,p.24.
12 Similarly in London the traditional music publishers and record companies found themselves competing overnight with a host of new rivals following the sudden success of British popular composers in the 1960's.

4 A page from the Sarum Missal, printed by Richard Pynson in London, 1500.

later. Until the introduction of statutory protection against unauthorised reproduction and performance, the remuneration of authors and composers appears to have been almost entirely the subject of outright sales to publishers, printers or producers. There is little justification for the performing right or other copyright prior to the eighteenth century, despite the arguments of Dr. Dock [13].

Soon after its invention the importance of controlling printing as a Crown prerogative was recognised in England. Under the Tudors, the notorious Star Chamber rose with authority to examine and convict which was foreign to the common law. By a decree of 23rd June 1585, the Star Chamber extended its influence firmly to the young art of printing. Thereafter every book had to be licensed, and this control continued until the abolition of the Star Chamber in 1640 [14]. While the Star Chamber extended its authority over the field of printing, an era of prosperity set in for the fortunate members of the Stationers Company. When it was abolished, both the decrees of the Star Chamber and the powers of the Stationers Company were at an end. Accordingly the Company petitioned in 1643 for greater powers of regulation. "Too great Multitudes of presses" set up by "Drapers, Carmen and others" were said to be indiscriminately at work [15]. The petition is of great value in the development of copyright history, for it speaks of the need to protect authors and assignees of copyright.

Thus "As it discourages stationers, so it is a great discouragement to the authors of books also: many mens' studies carry no other profit or recompense with them, but the benefit of their copies." And as to assignees "Many families now have their livelihoods by assignment of copies . . . and there is no reason apparent why the production of the brains should not be as assignable as . . . the right of any goods or chattels whatsoever" [16]. The Long Parliament restored the position by what was virtually a restatement of an old Star Chamber decree in 1643. By the *Licensing Act 1662* (*13 and 14 Car.II,c.33*) the printing of any book was forbidden unless first licensed and registered with the Stationers Company, and the old office of Licenser was revived. Sir Arnold Plant compressed neatly the history of the control existing until pressure for a copyright act built up in the United Kingdom [17]. The Licensing Act expired in 1679, was renewed in 1685, continued until

---

13 Marie-Claude Dock, Etude sur le Droit d'Auteur, esp. Titre Deuxieme.
14 Copinger and Skone-James, Copyright, 11th edn. para.23.
15 Edward Arber, op.cit., Vol.I.
16 Edward Arber, op.cit., Vol.I.
17 Plant, op.cit.,p.178.

1692, and then re-enacted for two more years. It lapsed finally in 1694, and with it the authority of the Stationers' Company to restrain printing ceased.

There are few references to music printing in the discussion of this licensing system. Part of the control was aimed at "heretical books and pamphlets", as in the *Licensing Act 1662* (supra), and music as such could scarcely contain anything offensive to the state. The ratio of music to prose would have been very small, at least until the eighteenth century. Much early printing of music would have been in book form, or even merely a page of printed music isolated among the conventionally printed pages of a prayer book[18]. Thus any music covered by early records may simply have been covered by the general term "books".

The London booksellers were by and large members of the Stationers' Company and therefore were champions of the licensing system. During the seventeenth century more booksellers sprang up in the provinces and in Scotland who were not members of the Company in most cases, and who began to flout the regulations increasingly, particularly after the lapse of the Licensing Act in 1694. The London booksellers made strenuous attempts to secure another Licensing Act. They petitioned Parliament on a number of occasions about their plight. "The liberty now set on foot of breaking through this ancient and reasonable usage is no way to be effectually restrained but by an Act of Parliament"[19]. Their efforts were successful in 1709 when they obtained the passage of the first copyright statute, the *Statute of Anne (8 Anne, c. 19)*.

By this, authors of books then printed were granted the sole right of printing for twenty-one years from 1710, and in the case of books thereafter printed the sole right of printing for fourteen years, with a reversionary right in favour of the author if still living after fourteen years. In the U.K. this was the turning point for authors' rights. Though the act referred in terms to books, musical and dramatic compositions were held to be books within the meaning of the act in *Bach v. Longman*[20].

Also from the Statute of Anne flowed throughout the nineteenth century the impetus for the piecemeal legislation now assembled into the *Copyright Act 1956;* at first only the rights of reproduction, and then with the *Dramatic Copyright Act 1833* and the *Literary Copyright Act 1842*, the performing rights which make up the main subject of this

---

18 A. Hyatt King, op.cit.,p.24.
19 4 Burr. 2318.
20 (1777)2 Cowp.623.

work. The Act of 1709 also led to the decision in *Donaldson v. Beckett*[21], which held that the common law copyright in published works had been extinguished by the act. According to Augustine Birrell[22], "but for the Statute of Anne, there might have been a perpetual copyright in England"[23].

Useful work has been completed on the remuneration of authors in France prior to copyright legislation there[24]. All the research is concentrated on literary and dramatic work, and the writer is perhaps over keen to find general acceptance of a performing right when the evidence points rather to isolated examples, but the conclusions are very similar to the practices found later in England by the Select Committee to enquire into the Laws affecting Dramatic Literature 1831-2.

According to Louis de Lomenie, the first French dramatist to make any financial gain from his work was Alexandre Hardy at the beginning of the seventeenth century[25]. He draws this conclusion from a sonnet written by Hardy himself. But according to the evidence of other commentators, Ruteboeuf sold a monologue to some strolling players as early as 1260[26]. The authoritative periodical Droit d'Auteur, on the other hand, attributes that distinction to a "Canon of Le Mans", who composed a mystery play about the Nativity, the Resurrection and the Passion, and sold it in Paris for fifty francs[27]. It is also known that the guilds of masons and carpenters in Paris commissioned Pierre Gringoire, a carpenter himself, to write a dramatic "Life of Louis, King of France", and paid him one hundred pounds for his work[28]. But these are all once and for all payments, and do not at all justify the comment of Dr. Dock that the references demonstrate the existence of a performing right in those times[29]. The essential element of payment repeated in respect of each performance is absent, as is the right of the author to control subsequent performances. It contrasts strangely with her observations shortly afterwards that "it was only from the time of Quinault in 1653 that a right to a proportion of the receipts was granted

---

21 (1774)4 Burr.2408.
22 Augustine Birrell, op.cit.,p.21.
23 To a certain extent there still is, for the effect of **S.2(3)Copyright Act** 1956 is that copyright in an unpublished musical, dramatic or literary work is perpetual so long as that work remains unpublished.
24 M-C Dock, op.cit.,especially pp.98 - 110.
25 Lomenie, Beaumarchais et son Temps, (1855), Paris,p.6.
26 Petit de Julleville, Les comedians de France en moyen Age, 1885,Ch.4.
27 Droit d'Auteur, 1903,p.96.
28 Petit de Julleville, op.cit.,Ch.4.
29 Dock,op.cit.,p.99.

to the authors"[30]. It is said that this author, when he was still unknown was refused by the company of the Hotel de Bourgogne the price which he had asked for the outright sale of his first play "The Rivals". To justify his faith in its success, he accepted as a compromise one ninth of the receipts for each night that the play ran, and it is said that thereafter this practice was widely adopted as a method of remuneration.

It was clearly not universal however. A French dramatic historian doubts that it existed at all at that time[31]. Chappuzeau contends that the most usual form of remuneration was for the author to take a share of the receipts while the play enjoyed a certain novelty value, but once this had expired he lost the right to a share[32]. Bonnassies puts forward a third theory, that the only gain for the author was the glory and the enhancement of his reputation[33]. This theory is shared in the U.K. by Sir Arnold Plant. "Speak to them on the subject of direct immediate return, and they reply in terms of numbers of off-prints or 'separates'. In just that way were authors quite generally remunerated in this country in the sixteenth century; they sold their manuscript outright to the publisher for perhaps at most one or two hundred copies: on occasion a little money might also pass"[34]. There is nevertheless a great deal of difference between a few off-prints of a short article of academic interest in the present day, and two hundred copies of say a new play, which properly bound and sold at perhaps eight per cent of the printer's ordinary selling price on the retail market might fetch a respectable sum for the author. There seems no more certainty in France than in Britain as to the most usual manner of remunerating writers prior to the eighteenth century.

In 1680 the Comédie Francaise was granted a monopoly of the theatre by letters patent, and this situation continued right up to the Revolution[35]. Thereafter fragments of the regulations have been preserved which demonstrate that the author had a voice in the price of admission to the theatre, since if the total receipts for a certain number of performances fell below a particular number, the author could seek a reduction in the admission charge, and thereby presumably hope for an increase in his share of the takings. Other records of accounts suggest that after the monopoly was set up, in the early days an author received

30 Dock,op.cit.,p.101.
31 Bonnassies, Les auteurs dramatiques et la Comédie Francaise aux XVIIe et XVIIIe siecles (1874),p.4.
32 Chappuzeau, Le théâtre francois, 1674, p.89.
33 Bonnassies,op.cit.,p.86.
34 Plant,op.cit.,p.169.
35 Dock, op.cit.,p.103.

a share of the takings in proportion to the classification of his work[36].

It is known that attempts were made in 1697 to regulate more satisfactorily relations between the theatrical company and their authors, but the exact terms have been lost, and are only referred to in later documents. In 1726 in respect of new five-act plays accepted by the Comédie the author was entitled to a share of two-eighteenths of the nett proceeds after deduction of expenses. The success of the production at the box office was the factor which controlled the duration of the author's entitlement to participate in the receipts, and is a crude, if limited, performing right. Disputes between authors and executants continued, and a ruling by the Conseil of 18th June 1757 attempted to fortify the procedure. Authors of accepted new works were to receive a ninth of the nett receipts after deduction of expenses in respect of five act plays, a twelfth for three act plays, and an eighteenth for those of one act. These payments were to continue until receipts had on two consecutive or three non-consecutive performances fallen below twelve hundred francs in winter, or eight hundred francs in summer[37]. But it was still a primitive form of a true performing right. The author was unable to forbid the performance of his work, and his right to participate in the proceeds was of a limited duration only. But it is a form of literary property nevertheless, and more highly developed than in Britain at the same time.

From this point, a determined lobby sprang up in France in support of a formal copyright law. It was led by two main spearheads. One was a school of legal philosophy which argued that authors' rights should be separated from the question of booksellers' privileges. Pamphlets were circulated in pursuance of these ideas, and among authors themselves an organised lobby ensured that the principle was constantly being considered by the Conseil d'Etat throughout the eighteenth century. It will be seen that these two factors were consistently missing from attempts to introduce copyright in this country. On the one hand the writers seemed quite unable to organise themselves into any effective group, or indeed to show much evidence of understanding what they could gain from copyright. On the other, well into the nineteenth century the question was usually considered with the interests of the book producers (later to emerge as the publishers) uppermost. They were in the van of any agitation, and accordingly any reforms were slanted in their direction[38].

---

36 Dock, op.cit., p.106.
37 Dock, op.cit.,p.110.
38 So far as musical composers were concerned, a right first obtained in 1842 was to remain almost totally unexploited by them until it became in the British publishers' interests to take the opportunities up in 1914.

In 1789 came the French Revolution, and the atmosphere of radical change had arrived. By a decree of the Assembly dated 9th July 1791 the authors' right of performance was set up. It was followed by a right of reproduction in a decree of 19th-24th July 1793. Having put the works of authors dead for fifty years firmly in the public domain, the nub of the reform came in Article 3 of the decree.

"Works of living authors may not be performed at any public theatre in France without the formal consent of the author in writing, on pain of forfeiture of the entire benefit of the performance to the profit of the author." At one stroke the author had been put in the position of controlling the performance of his compositions by forbidding its use until a satisfactory agreement for compensating him had been concluded[39].

In the next chapter the evidence given to the Select Committee to enquire into the Laws affecting Dramatic Literature 1831-2 throws some light on methods of paying playwrights in England in the eighteenth and early nineteenth centuries. Before this there is a certain amount of discussion in older law reports of the lot of authors at the hands of those who put on their works for gain. Unhappily the indications are sparse, and they tend to conflict. Moreover, some of the cases referred to are only reported at second-hand, as footnotes to a later case.

This case is *Millar v. Taylor* (*1769*)[40]. For present purposes its own facts are of no interest, but it contains references to and discussions of two slightly earlier cases, which indicate recognition that a right to control reproduction did not amount to entire control over the use made of the work. Such other uses could amount to performance, although this was not expressed in so many words. The cases are important because it appears to be taken for granted that an author would have no right to remuneration for any such subsequent use, and that it would be free to the purchaser of the book.

In Millar v. Taylor an injunction had been granted for printing the second part of a history by Lord Clarendon. His son let Francis Gwyn have a copy, and a dispute arose as to whether this conveyed a right to print and publish. The court was of the opinion that "Mr. Francis Gwyn might make every use of it, except the profit of multiplying in print". Said Mr. Justice Willes[41] "The book conveys knowledge, instruction or entertainment; but multiplying copies in print is quite a distinct thing

---

39 Dock,op.cit.,p.152.
40 4 Burr. 2303 (98 ER 201).
41 p.216 in the English Reports.

34

from all the book communicates. And there is no incongruity to reserve that right, and yet convey the free use of all the book teaches.''

Mr. Justice Aston continued "Can it be conceived, that in purchasing a literary composition at a shop, the purchaser even thought he bought the right to be the printer and seller of that specific work? The improvement, knowledge or amusement which he can derive from the performance is all his own, but the right to the work, the copyright, remains in him whose industry composed it''[42].

If Mr. Justice Aston had appreciated that there might be a commercial exploitation of such performance, would his answer have been the same? It is quite possible that he would have regarded it as belonging to the author until separately assigned, for his main interest was obviously in protecting the economic interest of the creator of the work. But at that stage the judiciary had no opportunity to foresee how the market for exploitation was to develop.

This is demonstrated when Mr. Justice Aston cites Mr. Justice Yates in *Tonson v. Walker and Merchant* (30th April 1752)[43]. "But when an author prints and publishes his work, he lays it entirely open to the public, as much as when the owner of a piece of land lays it open to the highway. Neither the book nor the sentiments it contains can be afterwards recalled by the author. Every purchaser of a book is the owner of it, and as such he has the right to make what use of it he pleases . . . If the buyer of a book may not make what use of it he pleases, what line can be drawn that will not tend to supersede all his dominion over it? He may not lend it, if he is not to print it, because it will entrench upon the author's profits.''

From this it might appear that the judges in these cases would have been opposed to a performing right in favour of the author, if they could have recognised it. But they could have no idea of the immensity of such a right in present day terms. When they consider the lending of a book within the purchaser's rights, this is the case today, both if such lending is between individuals, and at the time of writing, even if the lending is by a library. Moreover, they were considering prose books, in one case a history. The opportunity for public performance of such works was almost inconceivable before the introduction of broadcasting, and at that time the treatment of dramatic works written for stage production was quite different.

There were undoubtedly enterprising individuals among eighteenth century dramatic authors who in the absence of a satisfactory law were

---

42 p.222 in the English Reports.
43 p.234 in the English Reports.

quite capable of taking steps to guard their interests. The earliest case to deal with the protection of a dramatic author against an unauthorised performance of his play is *Macklin v. Richardson*[44]. It is surprisingly clear in its description of the conflict in the theatre, and the judgment is firm.

The plaintiff was the author of "Love à la Mode" which was performed by his permission at different theatres in 1760 and the following years, but was never printed or published by him. It was never acted without his permission, and when the farce was over, the author would take the copy away from the prompter. Two actors applied to the author to perform the play at their benefits, and he made them pay, on one occasion 20 guineas, and on another 30 guineas for one night's performance. The defendant, who was the co-proprietor of a magazine, employed someone to go the theatre and copy down the words of the farce from the mouths of the actors, and having corrected these notes, the defendant published the first act of the play in his magazine. The plaintiff sued for an account, and to prevent printing and publication.

On behalf of the plaintiff it was argued "That he was remarkably cautious to preserve this property to himself by not permitting it to be acted without his special leave, and by constantly taking the copy away from the prompter as soon as the farce was over, also by making two of the actors pay for the performance of it for their benefits. It was held that this unauthorised publication did the author great harm, and a perpetual injunction was granted. In passing judgment, Lord Commissioner Smythe observed, "Besides the advantage from the performance, the author has another means of profit; from the printing and publishing, and there is as much reason he should be protected in that right as any other author."

The decision turned on the question of publication, which is the reproduction right, but the case is of great interest for the practice and apparent acceptance of what amounts to a performing right by two actors who were sufficiently distinguished to have benefits of their own, and to be in a position to pay twenty and thirty guineas for the right to perform. It was accepted as unremarkable, not only by them, but also by the Court, and it is unfortunate that no judicial comment was passed on the practice. That it was not in general use at that time is demonstrated by the Report of the Select Committee to enquire into the Laws affecting Dramatic Literature[45]. But Macklin v. Richardson is evidence that some

---

44 (1770) 2 Amb. 694, 27 E.R. 451.
45 Reports, Committees 1831/2,vol.7.

dramatists at least purported to retain all their rights, without transferring any of the property to the proprietor of the theatre. In this case the author exercised the performing right in both facets of its modern operation, by both preventing general performances and charging for such performances as he was disposed to authorise. This is by far the clearest indication in case-law of a performing right at that time.

There is an oblique reference to dramatic rights in *Storace v. Longman*[46]. In the course of argument it was suggested that where a song was composed to be sung by a particular singer at the Italian Opera, all compositions so performed were the property of the house. The point was not considered at length, and Lord Kenyon simply declined to support this view. In holding that no private arrangement could interfere with the author's statutory reproduction right, he made no direct finding on the performing right.

Eventually in 1822 a case was heard which bore directly on whether an author's copyright embraced the right to restrain performance. The case was *Murray v. Elliston*[47]. Byron had written "Marino Faliero" in 1820, and by deed on 14th April 1821 had assigned "the tragedy and poem and copyright thereof, and the exclusive right of printing and publishing, and all benefit and advantage thereof" to the plaintiff for £1050. The plaintiff caused copies to be printed and published, and the defendant, who was manager of the Theatre Royal, Drury Lane, after the tragedy had been published, announced its performance, albeit altered and abridged. No permission had been given by either the plaintiff or Byron to the defendant to perform the tragedy in any way, but nevertheless the defendant put on a performance.

It was argued for the plaintiff that the only question was whether the performance of the play for profit could injure the copyright. The defendant argued that Macklin v. Richardson should be distinguished because that play had never been published, and it had there been held that the defendant could not employ a shorthand writer to take it from the mouths of the actors and then publish it. It looks as if counsel for the defendant had not appreciated that Macklin v. Richardson concerned the right to publish the play, while what was being considered in his own case was the true performing right. He argued that the acting of the play was something apart from the writing of it, with which the author had no concern. "Persons go thither, not to read the work, or to hear it read,

---

46 (1809) 2 Camp.26(note), 170 E.R. 1069.
47 106 E.R. 1331.

but to see the combined effect of poetry, scenery and acting. Now of these three things, two are not produced by the author of the work: and the combined effect is just as much a new production, and even more so than the printed abridgement of a work. There are many instances in which works published have thus, without the permission of their authors, been brought upon the stage. The safe rule for the court to lay down is that an author is only protected from the piracy of his book itself, or from some considerable imitation of it.'' This submission prevailed, and the court held "We . . . are of opinion that an action cannot be maintained by the plaintiff against the defendant for publicly acting and representing the said tragedy, abridged in manner aforesaid, at the Theatre Royal, Drury Lane, for profit.''

The significance of this case has been overlooked. Although it is cited briefly in nineteenth centry textbooks on authors' rights, it has for several editions past been dropped from the major works on copyright in English. Yet it was a clear decision that the *Statute of Anne 1709* gave the dramatic author a reproduction right only, and that once his work was published he had no performing right. It was undoubtedly one of the main reasons for the introduction of the statutory performing right for dramatic works in the *Dramatic Copyright Act 1833*.

Twenty-six years later in *Russell v. Smith*[48], Lord Denman said, "After Murray v. Elliston it seems to have been considered that publication to an audience was not within the provisions of the Acts relating to copyright. Consequently 3 and 4 Will.4,c.15 was passed[49], and in respect to dramatic literary property gave to authors the profits arising from publication by representing the piece on stage.'' So the view of the judiciary both before and after the passage of the first statutory right was that there had previously been no effective copyright, in the nature of a performing right, in Britain.

---

48 (1848) 12 Q.B.217,116 E.R.849.
49 Dramatic Copyright Act 1833.

3

The Campaign for a Dramatic Right and the Performing Right Legislation

There was nothing in the United Kingdom to compare with the steady pressure for a dramatic right which had built up in France in the course of the eighteenth century. Led by both legal commentators and the writers themselves, it had been crowned with success in 1791[1], and the new right was immediately converted into a fresh source of remuneration in the form of royalties.

Very gradually from the start of the nineteenth century, new factors in Britain began to work for a more satisfactory law on dramatic rights. Among these were social change and the spread of education. The expansion of the middle class and increasing standards of literacy greatly amplified the call for cheap and plentiful books, while the invention of new techniques demanded fresh kinds of protection[2].

The output and consumption of paper for printing is strong evidence of the current of change. "Between 1740 and 1744 Scottish mills produced a mere 80 tons of paper a year . . . this had risen to 390 by 1770-1774: there is then a three fold leap in the next twenty years (to 140 tons by 1796-1800) and a further doubling in the first generation of the nineteenth century (2400 tons by 1820-1824.) The last figure is thirty times as great as the first - it is a vivid shaft of light on three-quarters of a century of cultural and economic change"[3].

So in an age of awakening interest in the arts, there was witnessed the passage of a variety of statutes extending the range of copyright, generally as a result of pressure from those concerned with the commercial exploitation of the creation. A series of Acts in the eighteenth century brought protection for engravings - *Engraving Copyright Act 1734*, *Engraving Copyright Act 1766*, *Prints Copyright*

---

1 Dock,op.cit., livre troisième.
2 See generally, McFarlane, "British Copyright Law; A Summary". The Accountants Magazine, August 1972,p.388.
3 Dr. T. C. Smout, "A History of the Scottish People 1560-1830", p.251.

Act 1777 - and works of sculpture received protection in 1814 by the *Sculpture Copyright Act 1814*. The authors and playwrights were also aware that their French counterparts had obtained a new law, and they were anxious to try for the same benefits. But France in the previous century had been ripe for the radical changes which came about with the Revolution. Britain had made a huge effort during the wars against Napoleon. It had been a time of unity against the danger outside the realm, but it had also been a time of swift rises in the cost of living and increased taxes. It was the time of Luddite Riots, and they were followed at the end of the wars by slump and wide unemployment. Agitation was widespread, and the Government began to fear revolution in the guise of the radical movement for reform.

"The agitation which had shaken England since Waterloo issued from two quite separate sources - the middle classes, unrepresented, prosperous, respectable, influenced by the democratic ideas of the French Revolution, but deeply law-abiding in their hunger for political power; and on the other a bitter and more revolutionary section of working men, smitten by the economic dislocation of war and its aftermath, prepared to talk of violence and perhaps even to use it"[4].

When three Reform Bills had failed to pass into law in 1831 due to the opposition of the Tories and William IVth, popular excitement in the country grew intense and widespread demonstrations occurred. Revolution faced the established orders and rather than allow the peerage to be cheapened by the wholesale creation of new members of the House of Lords, the Tory members of the Upper House simply abandoned their opposition, and the *Reform Act 1832* was passed.

The country would never be quite the same again. "The slaves in the West Indies were finally emancipated in 1833. For the first time in English history the Government made educational grants to religious societies . . . The Poor Law was reformed . . . The first effective Factory Act was passed . . . The whole system of local government was reconstructed, and the old local oligarchies were abolished . . . Meanwhile, great forces were at work outside the House of Commons"[5].

Against this background Mr. Edward Lytton Bulwer asked for a Select Committee to enquire into the state of the laws affecting dramatic literature and the performance of the drama[6]. The request related mainly to the monopoly of the larger theatres, which had been created in

---

4 Churchill, History of the English Speaking Peoples,vol.4,p.35.
5 Churchill,op.cit.,p.35,vol.4.
6 Hansard's Parliamentary Debates,3rd series,vol.13,col.239,31st May 1832.

1737[7]. This curious provision, akin to the monopoly of the Comédie Francaise in Paris, restricted straight drama to the three patent houses of Drury Lane, Covent Garden and in the summer, the Haymarket. Otherwise all shows had to contain singing and music. "In fact, although the law was obeyed in theory, it was not carried out in practice, and many were the subterfuges that enabled the Act to be circumvented"[8].

But as a footnote to the call for an end to that monopoly, Mr. Sheil, one of Lytton Bulwer's supporters, continued, "The last question was - should not authors be secured some of the fruits of their success? A play is performed; it is eminently prosperous; the author receives a certain sum on the third, the ninth, the twentieth representation. Why should his emoluments end there? Why, as long as the theatre has a profit, should he not participate in it? Why should the managers of the provincial theatres be permitted to perform his plays, and allow him no portion of the receipts?"

A Select Committee was accordingly set up, with a general brief to enquire into the laws affecting dramatic literature; the greater part of its report concerned the monopoly of the patent theatres, but some of the evidence taken related to performance, and is of great value to a study of the ways in which dramatic authors received remuneration, if they indeed received anything, in the period before the Committee's deliberations.

That evidence was sufficiently convincing for the Committee to attach the following recommendations to its report. "In regard to dramatic literature, it appears manifest that an author is at present subject to indefensible hardship and injustice; and the disparity of protection afforded to the labours of the dramatic writer, when compared even with that granted to authors in other branches of letters, seems alone sufficient to divert the ambition of eminent and successful writers from that department of intellectual exertion. Your Committee therefore earnestly recommend that the author of a play should possess the same legal rights, and enjoy the same legal protection, as the author of any other literary production, and that his performance should not be legally exhibited at any theatre, metropolitan or provincial, without his express and formal consent"[9].

---

7 This continued the theatrical patents granted by Royal Charter in 1660 at the Restoration.
8 Eric de Mare, "London 1851", Folio Society,p.89.
9 Reports, Committees,1831/2,vol.7,p.1,para.7.

The Committee further suggested that "In regard to authors, it is probable that . . . a greater security in the profits derived from their success, will give new encouragement to their ambition and perhaps, (if a play is never acted without producing some emolument to its writer) may direct their attention to the more durable, as being the more lucrative, classes of dramatic literature"[10].

The evidence upon which these recommendations are based is fascinating. On one side were ranged the theatrical proprietors, whose interest would be adversely affected by the introduction of a dramatic right. On the other side stood the dramatists, who would undoubtedly gain from such a right. Among the names of those who came forward to testify are many which are today still familiar, and not surprisingly there was considerable divergence between the two pressure groups. Testimony of this nature is obviously partial; it was later to evoke the jibe from a Permanent Secretary to the Board of Trade, "Authors, who are the principal witnesses, are interested witnesses: printed controversy is therefore, on the whole, one-sided"[11]. Sir Arnold Plant, never a wholehearted proponent of copyright, added "It is rather like relying on articles in the daily newspapers for views on the waste involved in press advertising. Bias, and fear of bias, make an author's judgement on copyright a little unreliable. His readers must exercise particular vigilance"[12].

One of the most interesting sections of the evidence is that portion in which details are given of the systems of paying authors which were in force at the time. The details conflict as between one witness and another, and there are signs of diffidence on the part of theatrical managers about their various practices. But something akin to the system known at the Comédie Francaise in the days prior to a statutory right in France was recognised in a fairly general way in London.

Sometimes there was a formal contract between the management and the author; sometimes there was not. One was as customary as the other it seems. If there was a contract then it would be for the outright sale of the work. If there was no contact there would be payments made in respect of certain nights during the run[13]. On the other hand Thomas Morton, the author, thought that there was an old practice that where there was no particular contract struck between author and manager,

10 Reports, Committees, 1831/2,vol.7,p., para.8.
11 T. H. Farre, The Fortnightly Review, December 1878.
12 Plant,op.cit.,p.168.
13 Evidence of David Osbaldiston, Reports, Committees 1831/2 vol.7,p.97.

the author should receive £33-6-8d. for each performance. The practice had originated at Drury Lane, he thought, and in any case would only have applied to the patent theatres[14]. This view is not supported by the rest of the evidence. Captain Forbes, the proprietor of Covent Garden, whose account on this aspect of the matter must be authoritative, said the payments were made on fixed nights, and these undoubtedly began with the third, sixth and ninth nights, very much as in France[15]. Thereafter there would be another payment if the play ran to twenty performances, and another if it ran to forty, although this was an extremely unusual occurence. Morton confirms that these were the nights of the authors' benefit, though by all accounts the practice had its hazards for him. At these nights a notice might be put up at the box-office "For the benefit of the author." The author then had the receipts of that night, after deduction of expenses, which could be as high as £100 at the patent theatres. Causes totally independent of the play might seriously affect the takings at the door, a stormy night, or an illumination. As Morton ruefully observed, "I have often watched the clouds, very often"[16].

One drawback for the author was that he had to wait another eleven nights after the ninth night before he could expect another share of the receipts, and in order to avoid paying this, the proprietors would very frequently terminate the run on the nineteenth night[17]. This was most unfair to the writer, because only if the play was likely to go to as many as thirty performances would the run continue past nineteen nights. Indeed, according to Morris, it was only the writers of 'legitimate' drama who were fortunate enough to get an author's share on the third night. Those who merely wrote farce had to wait until the sixth night for a share, which was called "the author's night of the farce"[18].

Again, some proprietors would not make an outright purchase of copyright in any circumstances, but would pay the author a fixed sum until the publication of the play, it being agreed that the author would not publish it for a period of, say, three months. The *Statute of Anne 1709* had extinguished the old common law protection for unpublished works, which was in effect perpetual until they were published. The decisions in *Macklin v. Richardson* and *Murray v. Elliston*[19] followed

---

14 Reports, Committees 1831/2,vol.7,p.142.
15 Reports, Committees 1831/2,vol.7,p.111.
16 Reports, Committees 1831/2,vol.7,p.142.
17 Evidence of Captain Forbes,Reports,Committees 1831/2,vol.7,p.111.
18 Reports, Committees 1831/2 vol.7,p.150.
19 See Chapter 2 ante.

the old common law on publication. Naturally a theatrical manager at that time would expect that after publication of a play, his company would enjoy no protection against performance by other companies. As we shall see, in fact his rivals would seize the first opportunity to make a copy of a successful play.

While the copyright in an unpublished play might be respected in London, the managers of the country theatres did not hesitate to bring out their own productions of plays running in the Metropolis which had not been published. Managers, according to David Osbaldiston of the Surrey Theatre, always tried to take down a copy of a play, and then perform it at the earliest opportunity[20]. Copying was apparently a scandal in those times. "They send shorthand writers into the pits of the theatres now, and instead of the prompter getting that which was formerly considered his perquisite, they steal it without any ceremony at all, and it has become a kind of property among booksellers and adventurers"[21]. Mathews was the proprietor of the Adelphi, but was in favour of protection for authors, for he had suffered from infringements of copyrights that he had bought. At the time of giving his evidence, he said that four such plays were being acted in breach of his rights alone at other London theatres.

Douglas Jerrold was an author who had suffered considerably from this practice. A play of his was produced at a country theatre a fortnight after it had been brought out in London, and Jerrold had written to the country manager asking for some recompense. The manager had replied that he would willingly have given the author £5 for a copy of the play, had he not already paid £2 for a copy of it to "some stranger". Jerrold did not doubt who that stranger was. "There is an agency office where they are obtained . . . Mr. Kenneth at the corner of Bow Street will supply any gentleman with a manuscript on the lowest terms." Jerrold had offered to sell authentic copies of his plays because as he said, he suffered two injuries. In the first place, authors were not paid for their works, "and in the next place, they are represented by the skeletons of their dramas, so that as it was emphatically said by a sufferer, the author is not only robbed, but murdered"[22].

Apparently the agency of Mr. Kenneth would retail a copy to a country manager for £2 or £3, and while some London managers thought that their country brethren if challenged in the courts would be able to

20 Reports, Committees 1831/2,vol.7,p.97.
21 Evidence of Charles Mathews, Reports, Committees 1831/2 vol.7,p.166.
22 Reports, Committees 1831/2,vol.7,p.156.

plead such long usage that they might have got away without having to pay damages for the infringement, Moncrieff on the other hand took the view that if he went down to a country theatre where one of his plays was being performed without his permission, with a witness and a copy of the manuscript to prove his title, he could have brought an action to recover the profits of the performance, on the basis that the play had not been published[23]. He knew of the decision in *Murray v. Elliston*[24], and believed that this would act in his favour. What irritated the dramatists most was that the country managers would pay to the copying agency as much as £3 for an inaccurate copy, when the author would have been glad to come to terms for as little as £5.

Morris, who was the proprietor of the Haymarket in those days, had brought with him the old account books of that establishment, going back into the eighteenth century. For three separate farces O'Keefe received forty guineas each in the 1780s. Andrews at the same time was paid £64-10/- for a full length play, which was still in the repertory of the Haymarket in 1832. He could not say from the records whether these represented payments for outright purchase of the copyrights, or whether they represented the fruits of the sixth performance - the author's night of the farce. Morris was of the opinion that these figures at the end of the eighteenth century represented about one-third of the sums given to an author of the same calibre in the eighteen-thirties[25].

He does not take account of the considerable inflation which had been experienced in Britain during and after the wars against Napoleon. Having regard to the fluctuations in wages and prices at the epoch between the dates under comparison, the figures are not constant. "According to Silberburg's index of retail prices, the cost of living, in terms of commodities, rose by 87% between 1790 and the peak year 1813. It then fell very sharply, and in 1822 was back at the pre-war level. Thereafter it rose again, to a peak of 28% above that level, in the boom year 1825, and then it fell again, to only 6% above 1790 in 1829. In 1832 it was 9% above the level of 1790"[26]. It is unlikely that the incomes of professional people would have followed exactly the same fluctuations, and any rise in their income during these years would probably have been largely retained.

It must be said on behalf of the theatrical proprietors that for a legit-

23 Reports, Committees 1831/2,vol.7,p.175.
24 See Chapter 2 ante.
25 Reports, Committees 1831/2,vol.7,p.150.
26 G. D. H. Cole and Raymond Postgate,"the Common People",p.203.

imate drama paid according to the system of the author's nights, for a dramatic piece which terminated at about the tenth or twelfth night, the author could do very well, for he would receive between a quarter and a third of the gross takings of the run, less the expenses of the author's nights. According to Morris, Covent Garden had given the largest sum to an author of which he was aware, that was £1000 for the very successful "John Bull", which took altogether £16,000 at the box-office. This was probably an outright purchase of the copyright, and the best estimate of what a successful dramatist received is again provided by Morris. For the third, sixth and ninth nights of a five act comedy, O'Keefe received £102-12/-.[27]

On the author's side, Morton considered that the lowest price he got for the publication of a successful comedy was £80 or £90, as against a highest figure of £300. On the other hand, if the remuneration was left to the system of the author's nights, for a play running between ten and twenty nights something between £300 and £400 was to be expected[28]. There were other systems of payment for dramatic work. William Moncrieff told the Committee that he had at one time been engaged at a theatre on its staff as a kind of hack writer. He would receive a weekly payment, and was under contract expressly to provide plays at very short notice. If the theatre was at any time short of a play, he might have only twenty-four hours in which to write one for them. In a season he would write from four to six plays in this manner, and in about 1825 was paid some £10 per week for his pains[29]. At the same period, an agricultural labourer would expect about 8/- a week, and a skilled man about 26/-.[30] As Moncrieff would only have been working part time at the theatre, and for part of the year at that, he would seem to have been faring quite well, indeed perhaps better than a successful freelance, for he might take a salary of £500 in a year from this means alone.

Jerrold told the committee members of an experience which is still echoed today by copyright users. The argument is that there is no need for a performing right royalty because the performance itself gives benefit to the author through publicising his work[31]. Jerrold applied to Covent Garden for some remuneration for a work of his which was being

---

27 Reports,Committees 1831/2,vol.7,p.150.
28 Reports,Committees 1831/2,vol.7,p.142.
29 Reports,Committees 1831/2,vol.7,p.175.
30 G. D. H. Cole and Raymond Postgate,op.cit.,chapter XVII.
31 The record manufacturers in particular had to overcome this argument by commercial users of their records such as broadcasters in relation to their rights under **s.12 Copyright Act 1956.**

played there without his authority. He received a letter in reply expressing more than surprise at his request, and saying that its performance at Covent Garden had done Jerrold a great deal of good. "I have not yet discovered that," commented Jerrold acidly. "The reputation I acquired did not give me sufficient influence to get a piece brought out next season at Covent Garden"[32].

The country theatres were a constant source of complaint by the authors. Because of their remoteness in those days they probably felt fairly safe in infringing, and if challenged would no doubt have relied on long usage. The railways had scarcely arrived, the roads were appalling, and a journey across the Irish Sea so hazardous that Londoners would seriously consider journeying to Portpatrick in remote Galloway in order to take the shortest possible sea crossing to Ireland.

But they provided the chief source of entertainment for a large number of people in their catchment areas, where the provincial towns were effectively capital cities in their own rights. As such they had no competition and must have received large takings. The London managers and authors both thought they had means. Morris conceded that the large provincial theatres such as Bath, Norwich, Liverpool, Edinburgh and Dublin, might find it worth their while to pay a lump sum of £20 or £30 for the right to perform a play which had been successful in London. It would be their reluctance rather than their inability to pay which would make extraction of the money by the author difficult[33].

The author Jerrold felt that if he received 5/- for every performance of one of his plays at a country theatre, he would have received a considerable sum - certainly more than the £60 he received for his play "Black Eyed Susan", made up of £50 from the Surrey Theatre and £10 for a copyright, which could not prevent the play being performed by other theatres. Apart from running 150 nights at the Surrey, it played 100 nights at the Pavillion, 30 nights at Covent Garden, and also had runs at other London theatres such as the West London and the Olympic, to say nothing of theatres outside the Metropolitan area. £60 was as much as T. P. Cooke, a leading actor of the day, would expect for six nights acting at Covent Garden[34].

Moncrieff agreed with this, and said that if he had only 2/6d. in respect of each performance by a country theatre, his income would have been considerably augmented[35]. Planché thought that he ought to be in

---

32 Reports, Committees 1831/2,vol.7,p.156.
33 Reports, Committees 1831/2,vol.7,p.150.
34 Reports, Committees 1831/2,vol.7,p.156.
35 Reports, Committees 1831/2,vol.7,p.175.

receipt of about £100 per year in respect of country performances of his plays, and that this could be paid without detriment to their interests. In his view five guineas was not too much to ask of each provincial theatre which put on one of his plays, for as he put it, "It must have cost Mr. Murray as much to obtain a copy by a shorthand writer"[36].

These criticisms were a little disarmed by Richard Raymond, the manager of the Liverpool Theatre, whose evidence was balanced and very much in support of some aspects of the writers' case. He was not sure that he would be prepared to pay £20 for the right to perform in every case, but if the play would generate sufficient profit to make this worthwhile, he would go to that sum. Furthermore, he considered that provincial managers could afford a moderate payment for the right to put on a play after it had finished its London run, and that if the country theatres were prevented from putting on plays which had been brought out in London, there would be a great scarcity of new plays in the provinces. He saw no objection to an enactment giving such a right to authors[37].

All the evidence was centred on the position of the drama, and the only reference to musical composition was where it came in on the coat-tails of the drama. According to Captain Forbes, proprietor of Covent Garden, composers did not participate in the authors' nights, but simply received a payment for the copyright. As early as 1777 musical compositions had been held to be books within the meaning of the *Statute of Anne 1709*, in *Bach v. Longman*[38]. In the one example given, in respect of "Oberon", the author Planché had received £400, and the composer Weber had received £500 for the music[39]. There was no pressure from composers at this time for any form of performing right.

Perhaps the greatest influence which had caused an upsurge of interest in the chance of obtaining the new right in Britain was the knowledge among literary men of what their colleagues in France had obtained in 1791. During the campaign in France in the eighteenth century a commission for the defence of dramatic authors had been set up by Beaumarchais, Sedaine and Marmontel as early as 1777[40], and their initiative kept up the pressure during the years of the Revolution and after. Their efforts were crowned with the success of the law of 13th/19th January 1791, which was also the year of the new constitution, and the declara-

36 Reports, Committees 1831/2,vol.7,p.214.
37 Reports, Committees 1831/2,vol.7,p.209.
38 (1777) 2 Cowp.623.
39 Reports, Committees 1831/2,vol.7,p.111.
40 Pinner, World Copyright,p.447.

tion of the Rights of Man. If it should be thought strange that the founders of the new Republic should be responsible for the introduction of a new property right, it should be remembered that "in all these provisions there was nothing of socialism. The French Revolution attacked privilege, not property"[41].

Immediately after the new Act, a Dramatic Bureau was set up which was also a collecting agency, certainly in respect of dramatic works. Another Bureau was founded shortly after, and the amalgamation in March 1829 of the two agencies resulted in the foundation of the Société des Auteurs et Compositeurs Dramatiques. This undoubtedly had as its object the mutual defence of the interests of dramatic authors and the collection of their performing right royalties, but according to Pinner it also had some responsibility for composers[42].

This does not harmonise with the evidence of Chappell the music publisher given later to the Copyright Commission of 1875/6. He stated that "In that society (the Society of Dramatic Authors) musicians are excluded and on account of their exclusion another society has been formed of dramatic authors, musicians and editors (publishers), which has only been in existence for about fifteen years"[43]. That this is probably the more accurate account is confirmed by the historian of SACEM, the French performing right society of the present day[44]. Although the law of 1791 extended to musical works, promoters of concerts and other music users continuing to perform musical works without offering any compensation to the composers were causing considerable unrest and dissatisfaction among the ranks of the latter. They were also finding difficulty in keeping accurate accounts of all the occasions and places at which their works were performed[45].

As to the dramatic authors, La Porte explained that the playwright received a royalty in respect of each performance of his play in Paris. As the manager of French plays at the Tottenham Street Theatre his experience was extremely useful to the Select Committee. He told them that the theatres in the French provinces were divided into classes, and according to the size and importance of the town, so the amount of the royalty was decided, but nevertheless a separate sum was payable in

41 Fisher, A History of Europe,p.804.
42 Pinner,op.cit.,p.448.
43 Report (1878),p.109.
44 Lemoine,"La Societé des Auteurs, Compositeurs et Éditeurs de Musique 1850-1950",p.15.
45 The matter was to be remedied by actions brought in 1847 by the composer Bourget. These will be discussed in the next chapter.

respect of each performance. The author knew of the performances of his play, because there was an agency, presumably of one or the other of the Bureaux or of the Société, in every town in which there was a theatre. Therefore the royalties were collected regularly every year. The terms were apparently 12½% of the receipts, which in larger towns such as Lyons or Marseilles might yield about half of what might be expected in Paris., but the receipts in smaller towns would be less, for there was no government subsidy in those places. La Porte confirmed that in practice the right was not only to a royalty in respect of each performance, but the author also had the right to refuse altogether to allow a performance[46].

The system described by La Porte is in essence extremely similar to that now used by authors' societies all over the world, yet France was nearly one hundred years ahead of other countries in having any established society for the collection of performing right royalties, and her first society for the collection of music royalties was forty years ahead of the next to be formed. An Italian society was set up in 1883, an Austrian society in 1897, a Spanish society in 1899, a German society in 1903, and both a British and an American society in the same year, 1914. It was not until after the First World War that anything approaching a general international system was established[47].

The 1831/2 Committee was sympathetic to the authors, and asked witnesses for their views on what reforms could assist. Both Moncrieff and La Porte thought that the French system offered a ready example. According to the former, "nothing could be better than to adopt the French system of remuneration in Britain"[48]. La Porte thought that this would greatly encourage the production of plays of a more permanent nature, of more worth than many being produced at that time. There was some indication of unease among managers and proprietors about modish dramas which even then were clearly going to have no appeal beyond that generation of theatre-goers[49].

Others felt the most fruitful measure to be an assault on the country managements. Poole, another author, considered his income would have been increased ten-fold had he received anything from provincial theatres; he wanted a new law enforced by a system of agents in the prov-

---

46 Reports, Committees 1831/2, vol.7,p.126.
47 For a full account of the setting up of collecting societies across the world, see McFarlane, "Authors Societies", Grove's Dictionary of Music and Musicians, published by Macmillan.
48 Reports, Committees 1831/2,vol.7,p.175.
49 Reports, Committees 1831/2,vol.7,p.126.

inces, who would keep an account and collect the royalties due to writers[50]. This practical suggestion was supported by Douglas Jerrold, who considered that any legislative provision should be given teeth by making any infringing manager liable to a penalty[51]. This foreshadowed the Acts of 1833 and 1842. After the Committee reported, events were to move forward fast.

On 10th June 1833 the *Dramatic Copyright Act*, known after its sponsor as Bulwer Lytton's Act, received the Royal Assent. The terms of the Act are not widely known, and have not been printed in an English textbook on copyright since the last edition of Lord Justice Scrutton's work appeared at the turn of the century[52]. Because of its significance in this study, it is reproduced here in full.

"Whereas by an Act (54 Geo.3,c.156) it was among other things provided and enacted, that from and after the passing of the said Act the author of any book or books composed, and not printed or published, and his assignee or assignees, should have the sole liberty of printing and reprinting such books for the full term of twenty-eight years, to commence from the day of first publishing the same, and also, if the author should be living at the end of that period, for the residue of his natural life; and whereas it is expedient to extend the provisions of the said Act; Be it therefore enacted that from and after the passing of this Act the author of any tragedy, comedy, play, opera, farce, or any other dramatic piece of entertainment, composed and not printed and published by the author thereof or his assignee, or the assignee of such author, shall have as his own property the sole liberty of representing, or causing to be represented, at any place or places of dramatic entertainment whatsoever, in any part of the United Kingdom of Great Britain and Ireland, in the Isles of Man, Jersey and Guernsey, or in any part of the British Dominions, any such production as aforesaid, not printed or published by the author thereof or his assignee, and shall be deemed and taken to be the proprietor thereof; and the author of any such production, printed and published within ten years before the passing of this Act by the author thereof or his assignee, or which shall hereafter be so printed and published, or the assignee of such author, shall, from the time of passing of this Act, or from the time of such passing respectively, until the end of

---

50 Reports, Committees 1831/2,vol.7,p.190.
51 Reports, Committees 1831/2,vol7,p.156.
52 Scrutton, The Law of Copyright.

twenty-eight years from the day of such first publication of the same, and also, if the author or authors, or the survivor of the authors, shall be living at the end of that period, during the residue of his natural life, have as his own property the sole liberty of representing, or causing to be represented, the same at any such place of dramatic entertainment as aforesaid, and shall be deemed and taken to be the proprietor thereof: Provided nevertheless, that nothing in this Act contained shall prejudice, alter or affect the right or authority of any person to represent or cause to be represented, at any place or places of dramatic entertainment whatsoever, any such production as aforesaid, in all cases in which the author thereof or his assignee shall, previously to the passing of this Act, have given his consent to or authorised such representation, but that such sole liberty of the author or his assignee shall be subject to such right or authority.

If any person shall, during the continuance of such sole liberty as aforesaid, contrary to the intent of this Act, or right of the author or his assignee, represent or cause to be represented, without the consent in writing of the author or other proprietor first had and obtained, at any place of dramatic entertainment within the limits as aforesaid, any such production as aforesaid, or any part thereof, every such offender shall be liable for each and every such representation to the payment of an amount not less than forty shillings, or to the full amount of the benefit or advantage arising from such representation, or the injury or loss sustained by the plaintiff therefrom, whichever shall be the greater damages, to the author or other proprietor of such other production so represented contrary to the true intent and meaning of this Act, to be recovered, together with double costs of suit, by such author or other proprietors, in any court having jurisdiction in such cases in that part of the said United Kingdom or of the British Dominions in which the offence shall be committed; and in every such proceeding where the sole liberty of such author or his assignee as aforesaid shall be subject to such right or authority as aforesaid, it shall be sufficient for the plaintiff to state he has such sole liberty, without stating the same to be subject to such right or authority, or otherwise mentioning the same.

Provided nevertheless, that all such actions or proceedings for any offence or injury that shall be committed against this Act shall be brought, sued and commenced within twelve calendar months next after such offence committed, or else the same shall be void and of no effect.''

After the long struggle by the supporters of the performing right for dramatic authors, and the elaborate nature of the evidence given to the

Select Committee whose report eventually led to the 1833 Act, the subsequent extension of the concept to musical works is something of an anti-climax. Musical composers and their publishers did not band themselves together in the way that the supporters of the dramatists had, they brought no actions in the courts, and they did not lobby Parliament. The provision slipped through as a postscript to Sergeant Talfourd's Act - perhaps even as an afterthought.

Not that Sergeant Talfourd's Act had an easy passage. On the contrary, it was extremely bitterly contested at every stage, and Talfourd had to compromise very considerably in order to get the measure through at all. He first spoke to it on 18th May 1837[53], but not until 26th April 1842 did the matter receive the Royal Assent. The real issue was the extension of the period of copyright from that fixed by the *Copyright Act 1814* of twenty-eight years, or if the author were alive at the expiry of that term, his life. Eventually by his Act Talfourd achieved a term of forty-two years from publication, or seven years from the author's death, whichever was the longest.

Talfourd introduced the issue again in 1838[54], and numbered Disraeli among his supporters. It did not succeed in that year, or again in 1840. In 1841 Macaulay intervened in the debates, speaking to the House in terms which were clearly designed to become literature[55], but very much against the extension in any way of the period of copyright, drawing from Talfourd who saw himself defeated yet again the bitter jibe, "Literature's own familiar friend in whom she trusted, and who has eaten of her bread, has lifted up his heel against her."

Though he did not achieve the complete rejection of the Bill, Macaulay secured a considerable reduction in the term of copyright as there proposed. When introducing his Bill again in 1841, Talfourd proposed a period of sixty years[56]. This Bill was defeated by 45 votes to 38, the minority including Lytton Bulwer, Disraeli and Gladstone. Talfourd was raised to the High Court Bench before the next session of Parliament, and it was left to Lord Stanhope to introduce the Bill again[57]. He proposed a minimum period of twenty-eight years, and a general term of twenty-five years post-mortem. Macaulay countered with a term of forty-two years or the author's life, whichever should be the longest. His amendment was carried by 68 votes to 86[58], but against Macaulay's

---

53 1837 Hansard, House of Commons Debates,p.871.
54 1838 Hansard,xliii,557.
55 Macaulay's Speeches,108,109; also 1841 Hansard,li,341.
56 1841 Hansard,lvi,340.
57 1842 Hansard,lxi,1349.
58 1842 Hansard,lxi,1398.

5   *Portrait of Thomas Babbington Macaulay by F. Grant, 1853.*

54

protests, Sir Robert Peel proposed a further amendment that in any event there should be a further period extending for seven years after the death of the author in order to benefit his dependants, and this was carried.

The matter is well documented, and covers a period of five years, the debates being recorded both in Hansard, and in cornerstones of English literature. Macaulay's biographer was to write "never has any public man, unendowed with the authority of a Minister, so easily moulded so important a piece of legislation into a shape which so accurately accorded with his own views as did Macaulay the Copyright Act of 1842"[59]. But nowhere is there any discussion of the provisions slipped in as *Sections 20 and 21, Literary Copyright Act 1842.*

"20. And whereas an Act was passed (3 Will 4,c.15) to amend the law relating to dramatic literary property, and it is expedient to extend the term of the sole liberty of representing dramatic pieces given by that Act to the full time by this Act provided for the continuance of copyright. And whereas it is expedient to extend to musical compositions the benefits of that Act and also of this Act: the provisions of the said Act of his late Majesty, and of this Act shall apply to musical compositions, and the sole liberty of representing or performing, or causing or permitting to be represented or performed any dramatic piece or musical composition, shall endure and be the property of the author thereof, and his assigns, for the term of this Act provided for the duration of the copyright in books, and the provisions hereinbefore enacted in respect of the property of such copyright, and of registering the same, shall apply to the liberty of representing or performing any dramatic piece or musical composition, as if the same were herein expressly re-enacted and applied thereto, save and except that the first public representation or performance of any dramatic piece or musical composition shall be deemed equivalent, in the construction of this Act, to the first publication of any book. Provided always, that in the case of any dramatic piece or musical composition in manuscript, it shall be sufficient for the person having the sole liberty of representing or performing, or causing to be represented or performed, the same, to register only the title thereof, the name and place of abode of the proprietor thereof, and the time and place of its first representation or performance.

---

59 Trevelyan's Macaulay,vol.ii,p.133.

21. The person who shall at any time have the sole liberty of representing such dramatic piece or musical composition shall have and enjoy the remedies given and provided in the same Act (3 Will.4,c.15), passed to amend the laws relating to dramatic literary property, during the whole of his interest therein, as fully as if the same were re-enacted in this Act.''

The French as always had been more direct in their approach. It seems that the law of 1791 extended to musical works, but promoters of concerts and other music users continued to perform musical works without offering any compensation to composers, who were finding it impossible to keep an account of all the occasions and places at which their works were played. The matter was brought to a head in 1847 by the composer Alexandre Bourget, who, in the company of Victor Parizot, went to a café-concert at the Ambassadeurs in the Champs-Élysées. There they heard one of Bourget's works being performed, and when the time came to pay the bill for their refreshments, they declined, on the ground that the proprietor of the café had not paid Bourget for the use of his composition. They went further, and on 8th September 1847, obtained an injunction in the Tribunal de Commerce de la Seine against the proprietor of the Ambassadeurs in respect of the unauthorised performance of the works of Bourget[60].

The defendant broke the terms of the injunction, and was on 3rd August 1848 condemned in damages, this decision being upheld by the Court of Appeal in Paris on 26th April 1849. Encouraged by this success Parizot, Bourget and others began to set up a collecting society for musical works, and on 28th February 1851 the Societé des Auteurs, Compositeurs et Editeurs de Musique was set up[61]. By contrast the British reaction to the new won right was painfully slow.

''Forty shillings or the full amount of the benefit or advantage arising from such representation.''-*S.2 Dramatic Copyright Act 1833*. This penalty for unauthorised performance was slipped into the statute no doubt with the very best of intentions; it was to have far wider effects than the draftsman could ever have imagined, and in the end was to prove the greatest single impediment to the effective operation of the

---

60 Lemoine, ''La Societé des Auteurs, Compositeurs et Editeurs de Musique,1850-1950'',p.15.
61 Not until 1914 was the Performing Right Society set up in Britain, and the reasons for this will be examined in Chapter 5 post. So lax indeed were British composers and music publishers about the collection of their royalties that the French society SACEM was obliged to set up an agency in London in the nineteenth century for the collection of royalties earned by its own members.

performing right by the composers, authors and publishers of musical works. This however is to move on some forty years after the *Literary Copyrght Act 1842*, when steps had to be taken to counteract the operations of an astute entrepreneur named Thomas Wall.

The first reported case in Britain after the introduction of the statutory performing right is *Planché v. Braham*[62]. At this time by the 1833 Act the only performing right was that in a dramatic work, which included "any tragedy, comedy, play, opera, farce." By "opera" it is clear that only the words thereof are contemplated. The case arose from the fact that the plaintiff had written the English words for the music of Weber's opera "Oberon". In this form it had been performed at Covent Garden with the defendant Braham in the leading role. The defendant afterwards engaged another author to write a different English libretto for the same music, and he then performed the opera with the new words. But Braham still made use of the plaintiff's words as the vehicle for two or three of the most successful arias in the opera. In the absence of any other remedy the plaintiff sued under the *Dramatic Copyright Act 1833* for "performing at a place of dramatic entertainment a part of a dramatic piece of which the plaintiff was the author, without his consent." It was found that there had been a performance of part of the plaintiff's production, and the statutory penalty was accordingly imposed in respect of the unauthorised use of the words. Nothing could then be done about the unauthorised use of the music.

S.20 Literary Copyright Act 1842 however extended the benefit of the *Dramatic Copyright Act 1833* to "musical compositions", and the first reported case on the operation of that statute was *Russell v. Smith*[63]. There the plaintiff had the sole right of representing a musical composition known as "The Ship on Fire". He sued for the unauthorised performance thereof under *S.20 Literary Copyright Act 1842*. Two arguments were raised for the defence. The first was that the piece in question was a song, and accordingly not a musical composition within the meaning of S.20. The second was that the building in which the work was performed was not a place of dramatic entertainment. The justifications for these contentions were ingenious, and as the court sidestepped the issues raised, there was for many years thereafter much doubt as to whether they might be sound.

It was argued for the defence that by *Planché v. Braham* it was at least questionable whether the *Dramatic Copyright Act 1833* in the case of a

---

62 (1838) 4 Bing.N.C.17.
63 (1848) 12 Q.B. 217.

musical composition fixed any direct liability on a person giving an unauthorised performance in public of the author's words, if the music were not also used. This, it was said, was the reason for the introduction of the *Literary Copyright Act 1842*, which merely brought musical compositions within the operation of the 1833 Act. The later Act, so it was argued, was of no effect unless the 'composition' there referred to had the same dramatic character as the 'piece' or 'entertainment' referred to in the 1833 Act. Furthermore, the place of entertainment, it was said, had to be a 'place of dramatic entertainment', as this was undoubtedly a requirement of the 1833 Act, which the statute of 1842 merely extended to musical compositions.

The court unfortunately took the easy way out, and simply decided that "The Ship on Fire" was a dramatic piece, and accordingly the building in which it was performed became a place of dramatic entertainment. Therefore it was unnecessary to decide either of the arguments raised for the defence. This was one reason for the reluctance of the performing right owners for many years thereafter to exercise the right. There was considerable uncertainty following *Russell v. Smith* as to whether (a) a musical composition had also to contain a dramatic element, as in an opera or an operetta, and (b), whether the unauthorised performance had to be given in a theatre for the 1842 Act to bite. There was in this case also the interesting obiter dicta that the *Dramatic Copyright Act 1833* had been passed as a direct result of the decision in *Murray v. Elliston*.

Decided cases under the new law came in only very slowly, and it was clear that only the owners of the performing right in what were felt to be unarguably dramatic works were attempting to enforce that right. Another of the very few early cases was *Shepherd v. Conquest*[64]. Here the plaintiffs were the lessees of the Surrey Theatre, and brought an action against the defendant proprietors of the Grecian Saloon, which was admitted to be a place of dramatic entertainment, to recover 17 separate penalties of 40/- each under the *Dramatic Copyright Act 1833* for the unauthorised public performance of a dramatic work of which the plaintiff claimed to be the owner. It appears that the plaintiffs employed one Courtney to visit Paris to see two plays then being performed in that city, with a view to adapting them or other French dramas for the London stage. Such adaptation without further authorisation in itself

---

64 (1856) 17 C.B. 427.

would probably have been considered a breach of copyright under the treaty then existing with France. The plaintiff paid Courtney's expenses in France, together with a weekly salary of £2, and on his return Courtney wrote "Old Joe and Young Joe". There was a verbal agreement without any written confirmation that the plaintiffs should enjoy the performing right in London in any plays which Courtney wrote for them, while he should keep the sole right of performance outside London. The play was first performed at the Surrey Theatre on 31st October 1853, but on 24th July 1854 Courtney gave a written assignment of the copyright in the play to the defendant, who caused it to be performed at the Grecian Saloon. Courtney admitted that although there was no written contract between himself and the plaintiffs, he had verbally granted them the right of performance in London.

It was argued on behalf of the plaintiffs that as they had employed Courtney to write the play, by analogy with patents it became their property, or at least the performing right did in relation to performances in London. Furthermore, they contended, there was no copyright until it existed in the plaintiffs. The defendant replied that the plaintiffs had failed to show that they were the asignees of either the copyright or the performing right, and this view was supported by the court, which held that an assignment of rights under the *Dramatic Copyright Act 1833* must be in writing, and that the plaintiffs had no rights until they could demonstrate that they were the first owners of copyright. In this case, they said, the employer was not the author, but Courtney was, and as the plaintiffs had no assignment, they could not sue for an infringement.

Under the present law by *S.36(3) Copyright Act 1956* no assignment of copyright shall have effect unless it is in writing signed by or on behalf of the assignor, but where there is a contract of service by *S.4 Copyright Act 1956* the copyright vests in the employer. Had Shepherd obtained a written assignment he would probably have been held entitled to the copyright, for his terms for Courtney seem very close to a contract of service. While the *Dramatic Copyright Act 1833* did not in terms require a written assignment, there was good precedent for such a requirement in other laws of the time governing copyright in a variety of subjects. Thus the assignment of the copyright in an engraving had to be in writing, attested by two witnesses, *S.1 Engraving Copyright Act 1734*, and the assignment of copyright in a work of sculpture had to be by deed, attested by two witnesses, *S.4 Sculpture Copyright Act 1814*. Shortly after *Shepherd v. Conquest*, *S.3 Fine Arts Copyright Act 1862* stipulated that the assignment of a painting, drawing or photograph had to be in writing, signed by the copyright owner or his agent. Still later it was decided in *Leyland v. Stewart* [65] that the assignment of copyright in a literary work should be in writing.

No doubt the common law of the time had a bearing on the situation. Before 1875 the only method of assigning a contractual right at law was by novation, which required the consent of the debtor. The rule of equity was to permit the assignment of contractual rights, whether such rights were legal or equitable. If the right were a legal right, equity forced the assignor to allow the assignee to use his name in a common law action. The assignor had to be a party to such action in order to bind him at law. Eventually general statutory provision for the assignment of choses in action was introduced by *S.25(6) Judicature Act 1873*, but special provisions relating to assignments were clearly made in statutes themselves dealing with choses in action, such as the various copyright statutes prior to the Judicature Act.

65 (1876) 4 Ch.D.419.

4

The Copyright Commission 1875/6: its considerations of the Literary Copyright Act and the Dramatic Authors Society

By the mid-nineteenth century there was general dissatisfaction with the whole condition of the law of copyright. The restricted operation of the performing right was simply one area of this dissatisfaction, which led to the establishment of a Royal Commission to review the whole subject, which sat in 1875 and 1876 under the Chairmanship of Lord John Manners, with Anthony Trollope one of the Commissioners who played a prominent part. At the conclusion of their deliberations they handed down a searing indictment of the state of the law as they found it.

"The first observation which a study of the existing law suggests is that its form, as distinguished from its substance, seems to us bad. The law is wholly destitute of any sort of arrangement, incomplete, often obscure, and even when it is intelligible upon long study, it is in many parts so ill-expressed that no-one who does not give such study to it can expect to understand it. The common-law principles which lie at the root of the law have never been settled. The well-known cases of *Millar v. Taylor*[1], *Donaldson v. Beckett*[2], and *Jeffreys v. Boosey*[3] ended in a difference of opinion among many of the most eminent judges who have ever sat upon the Bench. The fourteen Acts of Parliament which dealt with the subject were passed at different times between 1735 and 1875. They are drawn in different styles, and some are drawn so as to be hardly intelligible. Obscurity of style, however, is only one of the defects of these Acts. Their arrangement is often worse than their style. Of this the *Copyright Act 1842* is a conspicuous instance."[4]

---

1 (1769) 4 Burr.2303.
2 (1774) 4 Burr.2408.
3 (1855) 4 H. L. C. 815.
4 Copyright Commission 1875/6, Report, paras.7-9.

The Report also dealt in terms with the performing right. The Commissioners observed [5], "It may be convenient, however, before referring to them more particularly, to notice a difference that exists between books and musical and dramatic works. While in books there is only one copyright, in musical and dramatic works there are two, namely, the right of printed publication and the right of public performance." This emphasises the unsatisfactory nature of the situation as it existed, and it is doubtful whether the extent of the concepts involved was fully understood at the time. A performing right apparently only arose in a dramatic work when it was performed on stage, so that a play reading for example would not have qualified [6].

The recommendations of the Commission on the performing right were as follows [7]. "With regard to the duration of copyright in dramatic pieces and musical compositions, we recommend that both the performing right and the literary right should be the same as for books. We further propose, in order to avoid the disunion between the literary and the performing rights in musical compositions and dramatic pieces, that the printed publication of such works should give dramatic or performing rights, and that public performance should give literary copyright. For a similar reason it would be desirable that the author of the words of songs, as distinguished from the music, should have no copyright in representation or publication with the music, except by special agreement."

This final recommendation that the author, or as he would be known today, the lyric writer, should, except by special agreement, have no copyright in his words has not found its way into the present law. It was no doubt based on the evidence given to the Commission by the publisher Purday, who took the view that the words of songs published at that time were of very little value in literary terms. He recorded that fifty years earlier music publishers thought so little of the talents of lyricists that none of them would make any payment for the words. He went so far as to suggest that the amount of labour which went into the writing of the words of popular songs in those days was so small in comparison with the work which had gone into the writing of the music that the lyricist should not enjoy a performing right in the words of non-

---

5 Copyright Commission 1875/6, Report, para.72.
6 Today by **S.2(5)(c) Copyright Act 1956** the reading of a play in public is undoubtedly a performance in public, and so is the reading in public of a book, whether its contents are a novel, a poem or a play.
7 Copyright Commission 1875/6, Report,paras.74,75.

dramatic music [8] Such a suggestion would find little favour with the modern lyricist [9].

The Commissioners took interesting evidence on the effect of the *Literary Copyright Act 1842*. It seems that following the first few cases the penalty of forty shillings imposed by *S.2 Dramatic Copyright Act 1833* had come to be regarded as the standard penalty for infringement of the performing right in any case in which judgment was given for the right owner or his assignee. Thomas Chappell the music publisher spoke of this [10]. It had been decided by the courts, he said, that the singing of a song was liable to a fee of £2 for each performance, just the same as if it had been an opera. It is not really clear whether the draftsman of the 1842 Act intended this only to apply to dramatico-musical works such as operas, but it does appear that the interpretation which was being put on it was that all musical works at this time were caught, if the performance were in a place of dramatic entertainment. The effect, according to Mr. Chappell, was that "a great many poor singers who perhaps scarcely get £2 for singing a song, have been charged £2 for singing it," and his view was that the only intention of the Dramatic Copyright Act had been to catch performances of operas. As he observed, £2 at that time was not too much for the performance of an opera. They could be produced by arrangement with the right owners, and were generally substantial productions put on by experienced men who would be perfectly well aware that they would be infringing the law if they did not pay the composer. By contrast, even today £2 would be grossly excessive for certain types of performance of the ordinary popular song, so Chappell may well have been correct in his surmise.

A number of the witnesses on the other hand suggested that a performing royalty of 6d. or 1/- should be payable, which would do away with the unwanted practices of freelance informers, who had been attracted to the field [11]. The common informer had for many years been known to English law, and a statutory penalty such as was provided for in the performing right legislation of 1833 and 1842 furnished a new and fertile area for exploitation. Undoubtedly it was from their ranks that sprang the notorious Thomas Wall [12].

---

8 Copyright Commission 1875/6, Minutes of Evidence,p.194.
9 Today author members enjoy equal status with composer members within the Performing Right Society, and their words are protected against both unauthorised performance and unauthorised reproduction in printed form.
10 Copyright Commission 1875/6, Minutes of Evidence,p.106.
11 Copyright Commission 1875/6, Minutes of Evidence,p.113.
12 See Chapter 5 post.

The common informer was defined as a private person suing for his own benefit to recover a statutory penalty under one of the numerous acts which in the past provided for such actions - Tranton v. Astor [13]. Examples existed in acts such as *5 Edw.3.c.5* [*Sale of Wares after Close of Fair*], *Sales of Horses Act 1555* and the *Seal Fishery Act 1875*. Although the system had its advantages in the days before a developed system of criminal detection had evolved, it clearly could lead to abuse, as it was to in the case of performing rights. By the *Common Informers Act 1951*, virtually all classes of common informer were abolished [14].

Arthur Sullivan, as he then was, took the view that the *Literary Copyright Act 1842* could be so interpreted that if a massed choir of 2,000 persons gave a performance at the Crystal Palace without authorisation, every one of the 2,000 plus each individual member of the orchestra as well would be liable to a penalty of £2, making a total of over £4,000 [15]. He also questioned whether the 1842 Act extended beyond theatres to performances given in less formal places such as concert rooms. As the matter was so uncertain due to the confusion following *Russell v. Smith*[16] he considered that the rule should be framed on a definite statutory basis, suggesting that it be construed in favour of the composer by making performances in any public room subject to a performing right.

The publisher C. H. Purday had no doubts on the subject. He was of the opinion that it had never been contemplated that a single song should be the subject of a performing right, not indeed any other musical work apart from an opera. On the contrary he considered that their composers would be glad for their works to be sung anywhere without prior consent and without a royalty for the sake of the publicity [17]. He would take this view because at that time it was the practice for music publishers to pay singers a certain amount to perform that publisher's new songs as part of the promotional effort, and Mr. Purday was not anxious both to lay out this sum and also to pay the composer a new royalty. Not until well into the twentieth century in fact did British music publishers begin to appreciate the enormous potential of income from the performing right.

The research into the 1875/6 Commission has thrown up evidence of the existence of sophisticated exercise of the performing right at a date far earlier than was hitherto imagined, and yields an invaluable insight to students of British copyright into the nineteenth century practice of

13 (1917) 33T. L. R. 383-385.
14 Halsbury's Laws of England, 3rd edn., vol.10,p.554.
15 Copyright Commission 1875/6, Minutes of Evidence,p.113.
16 (1848) 12 Q.B.217.
17 Copyright Commission,1875/6, Minutes of Evidence,p.193.

techniques of copyright collection which the administrators of the major British societies dealing with authors' rights at the present time believed to be of comparatively recent origin.

For although the owners of the performing rights in musical works had been extremely slow to take advantage of their new statutory rights, the dramatists of nineteenth century Britain had not been so slothful. John Palgrave Simpson, himself a dramatic author, told the Commission about the Dramatic Authors Society, of which body he was the secretary[18]. It had been formed in 1832, probably in anticipation of the new statutory right for dramatic authors in the *Dramatic Copyright Act 1833*. Perhaps the founder members had been in the powerful lobby which had fought so hard for the new right - we are not told. Undoubtedly they would have been influenced by the formation in France in 1829 of the "Dramatique", the Société des Auteurs et Compositeurs Dramatiques, which did have its own roots going back into the eighteenth century.

Later in the story of the development of performing rights in this country the emergence of the Performing Right Society (PRS) will be examined in depth, for it has by far the greatest income and power among the organisations in the U.K. exercising any form of performing right. The history of the other societies having some interest will be traced in, such as Phonographic Performance Limited, (PPL), and the Society of Authors, whose parts are smaller by far. I had the advantage of working in the field of performing rights for some four years, three of them with PRS itself, and for three years served on the British Copyright Council. In all the discussions I have had on the issue with the leading figures in the practical work of collecting copyright royalties, no one had any notion that a society such as the Dramatic Authors Society had existed, and no organisation that I have contacted in Britain or abroad has any record that it existed.

What Mr. Simpson had to say is therefore of paramount importance to the subject; the striking parallels between the practices of his society and modern organisations can be made most clearly by footnotes at this stage of the study.

For it is a surprising fact that the Dramatic Authors Society had set up in Britain very advanced machinery for the collection and distribution of its members' royalties at an early date [19].

---

18 Copyright Commission, 1875/6, Minutes of Evidence,p.120.
19 But while today the annual turnover of PRS is over £10 million, the Dramatic Authors Society has ceased to exist. The rights in dramatic works are now either administered individually, or as a sideline to main work of the Society of Authors, which certainly does not regard its main function as that of a collecting society.

The Dramatic Authors Society was an organisation electing as its members any author who had one of his works produced in a theatre of standing, the society existing for their mutual protection. It collected the fees for the performances of the plays controlled by the Society from London managers, country managers, and even amateurs. London managers paid a fixed sum laid down by a tariff for each play, but this was found not to work in the country. There because of evasion, a system had been adopted whereby the country managers paid a fixed sum for the entire season for the privilege of performing the Society's plays. They then had to make a return to the Society of all their playbills for the season as a term of their contract with the Society. These were then analysed, and the receipts distributed among the authors whose works had been performed according to their entitlement, less a deduction of 10% for administrative expenses [20].

The Society had originally been formed as a result of the difficulty which dramatic authors had experienced in collecting their fees, but even after its formation, due to the evasion of the country managers, the income of the Society did not amount to much more than £800 a year. Then however the country managers were obliged to pay a set sum for the Society's licence, its income increased substantially, and by 1876 was varying between £4,000 and £5,000 per annum [21]. This was a considerable sum for those days, particularly having regard to there being no more than 99 members in the Society then controlling only some 2,000 works [22]. The provincial managers were obliged to pay in advance for their licences, and where it was found that country managers were performing works controlled by the Society without permission, the Society would bring proceedings under the *Dramatic Copyright Act 1833* for the statutory penalty of £2 in respect of each separate performance.

But the Dramatic Authors Society apparently found difficulty in bringing these actions, whether in the County court or the High court. It was obliged to bring actions, in so far as it could not allow infringements to pass unchallenged. But the cases took time to bring to court, and by then a travelling company would undoubtedly have moved on. Even when a verdict was obtained, the manager often proved to be a man of straw.

---

20 This is precisely the method employed to this day by PRS in respect of certain of its tariffs, as for example dance halls, and the returns of works performed are an important part of the analysis of entitlement upon which the members receipts are based. Due to certain human frailties reflected in the system of returns, it is not the entire basis of assessment.
21 Copyright Commission 1875/6, Minutes of Evidence,p.120.
22 Copyright Commission 1875/6, Appendix VIII.

Simpson estimated that the Society was losing between £500 and £600 per annum as a result of these evasions. His view was that penalties for unauthorised performance should be brought within the summary jurisdiction of the magistrates courts [23].

A further difficulty was that *s.2 Dramatic Copyright Act 1833* only extended to the person who "represents or causes to be represented." This presented another obstacle for the Dramatic Authors Society, for liability accordingly only extended to the manager of the theatrical company which had infringed. Only very rarely in those days was the manager of a company the lessee or proprietor of a theatre. More often he was a peripatetic individual who travelled around the land with his company, seldom if ever being a person of sufficient financial standing to meet any award of damages. His engagement with the theatre would often be simply for the week of the infringement before he moved on again, and an action against such a person would be quite futile. As Palgrave Simpson pointed out with feeling [24], it would have been a more satisfactory position for the Dramatic Authors Society if it had been able to take proceedings against the proprietor or lessee of the permanent establishment. In such actions as were brought, the Society was always put to strict proof of the authorship of the infringed work, which often caused difficulty and embarrassment [25].

Simpson was asked by the Commission whether the Dramatic Authors Society was able to sue as a corporate body. He replied that some years previously a charter of incorporation had been applied for, but had been refused because, although a corporate body, the Society sued for individual interests [26]. The Society also applied for permission to be registered under the *Friendly Societies Act 1875* in order to sue in its own name, rather than that of an individual author using an attorney. A very surprising reply was received by the Society from the Lords Commissioners of the Treasury. "Their Lordships desire me to inform you

---

23 There is now a criminal offence in **s.21(5) Copyright Act 1956,** introduced there for the first time, but it is not the policy of PRS or any other collecting organisation to take criminal proceedings for unauthorised public performance. This policy has not always been unanimously approved by those having the conduct of the affairs of PRS, some taking the view that the vigourous pursuit of infringers in the criminal courts would be likely to discourage the more blatant offenders. The others fear public opinion.
24 Copyright Commission 1875/6,Minutes of Evidence,p.121.
25 It still does today for PRS in the Chancery Division, particularly where title is vested in someone outside the U.K.
26 By contrast, PRS immediately upon its formation in 1914 was incorporated as a company limited by guarantee, and has always sued in respect of the individual interests assigned to it.

6   *A licensing representative for the PRS with a publican customer.*

that they are unable to comply with your request (to register the Society under the *Friendly Societies Act 1875*), inasmuch as it appears to them that the purposes of the Dramatic Authors Society are sufficiently in restraint of trade to render it capable of being registered under the *Trades Union Act 1871*, and a portion under the Amendment Act lately passed." Thus already by 1876 Government was sensitive to the monopolistic potentialities of collecting societies, a problem which has raised difficulties in many states since then.

Naturally, the system of detecting performances of its members' works in the mid-nineteenth century was close to that employed a century later by the musical collecting societies. Simpson organised a number of agents at the larger towns throughout the country, who would check on the various places of dramatic entertainment and report on any unauthorised performance [27].

The Dramatic Authors also scrutinised the theatrical paper of the day, "Era", which advertised details of performances at provincial theatres. This is the method used today by Phonographic Performance Limited (PPL), which collects on behalf of the performing rights in gramophone records. PPL is not large enough to afford a staff of provincial representatives and so, at its London headquarters, both local newspapers and the journals of the music industry are examined for advertisements and reports of establishments which might be using recorded music. The Dramatic Authors Society was also simply scrutinising the veracity of the returns which licensees were obliged to make as a term of their contract with the Society. Finally it seems that they simply also received information from people who had been aggrieved by the manager who was responsible for a particular infringement.

The Dramatic Authors Society found, as other societies were later to find, that there was difficulty in imposing its terms upon amateur dramatists. Prior to the 1833 Act, they had not made any payment at all, but thereafter they were required to do so by the Society, whose officers thereafter became the targets of abuse and insulting letters, generally along the lines that actors who had bought a copy of a play could not thereafter be expected to pay again for the performance. The difference between the publishing right and the performing right was still less well understood then than it is today.

---

27 PRS has field representatives carrying out much the same function. They require a background of detecting experience and considerable tact and are frequently drawn from the ranks of retired policemen. They have a much wider scope, for they have to cover not only "places of dramatic entertainment", but any establishment of a public nature where live or recorded music might be performed, for example shops.

Duck v. Bates[28] was to establish in the next decade that under the pre-1911 law a performance need not be for profit to bring the performing right into play, and this was followed in applying the *Copyright Act 1911* in *Jennings v. Stephens*[29]. But according to the evidence of Palgrave Simpson the matter had been dealt with in a case prior to *Duck v. Bates* which had been unreported[30]. "It has even been decided by law that if amateurs, forming a society or club, subscribe among themselves to get up a dramatic entertainment they are as liable to pay the fees for the authorship as if they received money at the doors. We have had the opinion of Mr. Brown Q.C. upon the subject, which opinion is printed and sent out to amateurs. In one case we were resisted by the City Artillery, who used to give performances in their own drill shed, and gave all the tickets away to their friends: it was decided that as long as they raised the money among themselves to pay the expenses of their dramatic entertainments they had as much right to pay the authors' fees as to pay their carpenters or scene shifters or scenic artists, or their orchestra or the ladies engaged to play with them - that was decided." The matter had been decided before Palgrave Simpson became secretary of the Society, and he did not know whether it had come before a County court or a higher court, but he presumed that it had been given in the form of a judgment.

Another surprise from the evidence is that at this early stage in the development of copyright collecting societies, the Dramatic Authors Society was attempting to enforce its rights in the then British Dominions[31]. According to Simpson, the Society took the view that the Acts enshrining the performing right in Britain applied equally in Canada, Australia, New Zealand and India, and they had appointed agents for the purpose of collecting their dues in those countries[32].

It had not met with much success apart from in Australia, where the agent was a "Senator" who received a commission of 35% on his receipts[33]. For a time he brought in a great deal of money, but then it seemed that litigation whittled away his achievements. Judgments began to be given against the Society, based on the view that no assign-

---

28 (1884) 13 Q.B.D.843.
29 [1936] ChD.469.
30 Copyright Commision 1875/6, Minutes of Evidence,p.122.
31 Only gradually and with painful difficulty did the PRS build up its overseas agencies in the British territories.
32 Copyright Commission 1875/6, Minutes of Evidence,p.123.
33 He could not have been a Senator, as the Australian Senate did not come into being until the various colonies were subsequently united. He was probably a member of one of the colonial upper Houses.

ment of a play was valid without proof of registration. Simpson contended that Parliament had specifically stated this requirement not to be necessary. Certainly the *Dramatic Copyright Act 1833* was expressed to extend to "any part of the British Dominions", and s.2 appears to state that in proceedings in any court of the British Dominions it was sufficient for the plaintiff to state that he enjoyed "the sole liberty". The true intention of the British legislature is not clear, but it may be an attempt to match the effect of *s.20(1)(b) Copyright Act 1956* in today's law.

In the absence of any rate-fixing body of the nature of the Performing Right Tribunal, a committee of the Dramatic Authors Society fixed the tariffs for that organisation - as Simpson observed, just like any other tradesmen fixing the price for the commodity they dealt in. Having assessed a theatre, they would insist on the management paying their account quarterly in advance, before the Society would grant its authority. Where a theatre nonetheless infringed the performing right, the Society would take action in the name of the author concerned, and would sue for the minimum penalty of £2. *S.2 Dramatic Copyright Act 1833* provided "Forty shillings or the full amount of the benefit or advantage arising from such representation", so that in effect the aggrieved author was theoretically entitled to all the benefit arising from the unauthorised performance of his work. However the Dramatic Authors Society in London took the view that it would be very difficult to prove the benefit derived, and as they were never able to get at the theatre's books to elicit the benefit arising from any performance, the Society made a practice of not seeking more than the minimum penalty. They did not apparently ask for discovery of the books, but this may have been due to uncertainty on the part of their advisers as to whether s.2 was an expression of fixed damages in civil law, or rather in the nature of a criminal penalty.

Its Australian agent had been more enterprising. He was a man of some versatility, for apart from his political activities, he had been a theatrical manager. Armed with the knowledge he had acquired in that capacity, in the days when he had been able to enforce the right successfully in Australia, he had generally gone for the benefit derived from the unauthorised performance, which sometimes amounted to 100 times the minimum penalty of £2. No doubt the commission of 35% provided the incentive for this enthusiastic interpretation of the Act.

The Society's receipts were divided by analysis of the playbills returned by the licensees as a term of their contracts. The number of performances of each play would be noted, and then a system of point rating was applied. A one-act play might attract one point, a two or three act play four points, and a five act play six points. The points would be multiplied by the number of performances, and that would go forward as the amount of entitlement when the sum available for distribution was divided up.

Infringers attempted to bribe the Society's agents, who were paid a commission of 10%. Simpson does not tell us if they were successful. They also attempted to bribe the editor of the stage newspaper "Era" not to print reports of performances of works controlled by the Society, but happily for that organisation the editor proved incorruptible.

According to Simpson almost every dramatic author of the day belonged to the Dramatic Authors Society, but not all did[34]. Some remained outside, and attempted to collect their dues by their own efforts, which was time-consuming and counter-productive. Others used an agent as has become the general case today. This is because in the case of a play, it is comparatively simple to earmark the various theatres using a play, and collect from them. Simpson relates that Boucicault and Gilbert both chose to stay outside, and thus were not bound by any tariff, being therefore free to demand the best rate that they could get from the user. Although no doubt it gave them more administrative trouble, both writers found such a scheme more remunerative because of the popularity of their productions.

Simpson also disclosed that, apart from dramatists, his society also numbered among the members two composers of music. Curiously, they had both given instructions that the Society was not to attempt to collect on their behalf in respect of single songs, but only to claim a royalty for operatic selections. Both composers apparently took the view that it would be to the disadvantage of sheet music sales to try to collect for single songs. Palgrave Simpson did not altogether agree with this view, and felt that it would be in the interests of the composer to claim a performance royalty for the singing of a single song. He implied that he would have liked his society to be the vehicle for the collection of such royalties. But as will be seen from the next chapter, a more enterprising hand was already embarking on the exploitation of this source of revenue[35].

---

34 Copyright Commission 1875/6,Minutes of Evidence,p.125.
35 While almost every British composer today belongs to PRS, at least 20% of its UK income is earned by its top 5 or 6 composers. Administrative expenses of some 11% are applied equally to all members, but the true cost of collecting each pound is much greater in the case of low earning members. If the top six composers earn say £1,000,000 p.a., the true cost of collecting this would be very much less than £100,000. If they chose to set up their own society or to collect individually they could seriously damage PRS, and remove much of the justification for the Performing Right Tribunal.

There is no doubt that under the present law, play readings attract a performing right royalty, and if detected, this will be exacted just as will be a royalty for the performance of a poem by reciting it. The Dramatic Authors Society had considered the position of play readings under the *Dramatic Copyright Act 1833*, and had come to the conclusion that the statute did not extend so far. There does not appear to have been a case on the point, but it looks as if the Society had taken counsel's opinion, for Simpson complained that a man could get up at a play reading and recite long passages from a play, and the law did not touch him. If two persons came together to recite a dialogue from the same play however, the Society considered them to be caught by the Act, even if they did so without scenery or costume or other such accessories [36].

The Act spoke not of "performing", but of "representing"; however the distinction does not appear to justify the conclusion drawn by the Society. A play is performed equally whether there are distinct actors for each separate part, or where one man reads aloud the whole. To hold otherwise would not admit to the benefit of the performing right the performance of a play of say ten parts, where five actors share the parts between themselves. Nor would it extend to the performance of a one-act play containing only one speaking part.

The Commission was concerned about imposing a strict liability on the proprietor of a theatre for any unauthorised performance of a play given at his establishment. Simpson sought to allay their fears by telling them that every owner or manager of a theatre licensed by the Society was sent a copy of the Dramatic Authors Society List, which clearly stated which works were controlled by the Society. He added that theatrical proprietors frequently wrote to him to enquire whether companies which they were proposing to engage had cleared their rights with the Society [37].

The evidence of Palgrave Simpson is invaluable to this study, for it fills the hitherto unaccountable gap between the introduction of the performing right in legislation in the early nineteenth century, and the apparent ignorance of the right which seemed to exist among the creative community of Britain until well into the twentieth century.

---

36 Copyright Commission 1875/6, Minutes of Evidence, p.125.
37 PRS does not claim to be able to supply a list of all the works which it controls, nor could it today possibly do so. The number of musical works extending virtually throughout the world which are linked to it through its affilliated societies abroad is not susceptible of calculation or statement at any point in time. Therefore PRS issues a blanket licence for the performance of any of its works (with certain very limited exceptions.) (This is some justification for the monopolist.)

Although no one in the copyright world today was aware of the earlier existence of the Dramatic Authors Society, it now seems possible that the techniques used by the modern organisations such as PRS and the Mechanical Rights Society in their early days were not necessarily borrowed from the French models or evolved by their first administrators, but may have derived from some dimly remembered operations of a defunct Dramatic Authors Society. But when and why it became defunct nobody is now able to say [38].

There is hardly any contemporary evidence available from composers as to why they were not trying at that time to exercise their rights, or indeed as to whether they were even aware of them. Sir Arthur Sullivan gave some views of his own to the Commission, but it is doubtful if they are typical of the great body of creators of music in Britain at that time. A number of music publishers though did testify, and their evidence demonstrates that there was both confusion, and a feeling that the publishing community at least would be more prosperous without the performing right in non-dramatic works.

For although the present day music publisher regards the proceeds of the performing right as a substantial part of his income, and takes a share of up to 50% of any royalties, the great publishers of the eighteen seventies had not recognised its potential. John Boosey, whose publishing house was to remain a leading influence on the world of music in the form of Boosey and Hawkes, admitted that he was aware of the success of the French collecting society, but recorded that no one whom he had met had showed the slightest desire to exercise the performing right. This was, he explained, because the money made by publication, which was much larger in England than in France, was so good that the composers were satisfied with it, and they considered that if the performing right were exercised, it would seriously interfere with the profits accruing from publication. He said that if a composer were making £500 at that time from a song over a six month period, he would be indifferent to any sums arising from the performing right, which Boosey naturally assumed would be very much smaller. Of course, he did not then forsee the decline which would come about in the sales of sheet music, due to technical developments [39].

It was put to him that the law was providing for the composer, his widow and heirs, not over a six month period but a considerably longer

---

38 Simpson's evidence is also of some philological interest. As late as 1876, both lawyers and literary men were using the words "piece" and "represent" where "play" and "perform" are now commonly used.
39 Copyright Commission 1875/6,Minutes of Evidence,p.102.

time, and that music users might well not object to paying a moderate sum in respect of the right. Boosey replied that although they might indeed raise no objection to such a payment, he considered that the whole body of composers would announce that they had waived their claim in such circumstances. He claimed that composers were in the habit then of paying singers handsomely to sing their songs, and that as they attached so much importance to the advertisement deriving from such performances, the composers would not dream of exacting a royalty for that performance. This is something very similar to the practice of "payola", and it may be that publishers were also handing out largesse in order to secure the performance of their published works. Certainly this was their practice towards the end of the century, when it is known that their budgets included substantial provision for the nation-wide performance of their songs[40].

Some publishers contended that the performing right was never really intended to extend beyond dramatic works, or operas at the very most. C. H. Purday argued that, far from composers seeking royalties in respect of performances, they would on the contrary welcome the performances in order to have greater recognition for their works[41]. What could be realised from the sale of the song was far more profitable than the chance of a penalty of £2, and that penalty itself was more probable to discourage potential singers. Speaking as a publisher, Purday said that he would be glad to see the performing right repealed, as this would give the work greater promotion. It would also end the situation whereby publishers paid the singer to sing the song as part of the promotional campaign, and the composer then received a performing royalty for that promotional singing[42].

Despite the rather hazardous chances of recovering a royalty for a performance in the United Kingdom, a British publisher when taking the rights for an opera written by a foreign composer would not only pay him for the copyright, but would also pay him a sum in respect of each night that the work was performed in this country, according to Boosey[43]. He

---

40 Today the International Federation of the Phonographic Industry (IFPI), whose brief is to promote on a world-wide basis the performing right in gramophone records, has suffered embarrassment as a result of some members resorting to "payola". Opponents of its rights can then claim that the performance is actually providing a service to the copyright owner.
41 Copyright Commission 1875/6,Minutes of Evidence,p.193.
42 Nowadays publisher and composer share the performance royalty, and neither pays for the singing of the song.
43 Copyright Commission 1875/6,Minutes of Evidence,p.100 et seq.

7   Portrait of Sir Arthur Sullivan by J.E. Millais, 1888.

was emphatic that while composers were not anxious to enjoy the performing right, he was equally certain that the publishers did not want to exercise it if it were offered to them. The fact that composers were so satisfied with their receipts from publishers that they did not seek any remuneration from performance he attributed to the fact that the amount paid to them by publishers had increased vastly over what had been paid at around the time when the performing right had first been set up by statute.

Another famous publisher, Chappell, inclined to the view that the performing right at that time probably extended to separate musical works and songs, but thought that the point had not really been decided, and in any case was effectively in abeyance. In order to protect himself if it should ever become an effective right for songs, he had since about 1860 when contracting to buy the copyright in a popular song included in the contract the words "and the right of performing the same". He considered that so far as small rights were concerned, it would not be worthwhile attempting to collect them except through the medium of a society, and he forsaw that if such a society came into existence, licensees would pay in a lump sum for a number of songs, the forerunner of the blanket licence.

The distinction between grand rights and small rights has always been of importance in the music industry. Often termed "grands droits" and "petits droits", the difference arose in this country from the requirement for a dramatic element in the performing right legislation of 1833 and 1842. On the one side stood the works having a dramatic element, such as opera, operetta and pantomime, the grand rights, and on the other, the musical works not having such a dramatic element, such as mere ballads which could be performed at a concert hall, in a hotel foyer, or at a *thé dansant*. These were known as the small rights, and at the time of the 1875 Commission the performing right seemed to be almost entirely exploited in the case of the grand rights. But no one seemed to want to push the matter to a conclusive decision.

Arthur Sullivan had on one occasion tried to prevent the performance of a non-dramatic song of his in a theatre which was undoubtedly a place of dramatic entertainment within the meaning of the statutes. He had been able to prevent the matter by negotiation, but expressed some doubt as to whether the situation was really covered by the application of the *Dramatic Copyright Act 1833* and the *Literary Copyright Act 1842*[44]. The Commission agreed with his further proposition that there was con-

44 Copyright Commission 1875/6,Minutes of Evidence,p.110.

siderable doubt as to whether these Acts gave the composer of a non-dramatic song the right to prevent its performance in a venue which was not a place of dramatic entertainment. This power is obviously important to a serious composer, for example in the case of burlesques.

He also felt that there was considerable doubt on the point of whether there existed any kind of performing right in non-dramatic songs. In his publishing contracts at least the question of the transfer of the performing right was never referred to, but apparently a custom had grown up in the trade that the transfer of copyright at that stage also transferred the performing right. Sullivan however wished the composer to retain some kind of moral right to restrain the performance of one of his works in an unsuitable environment, and objected in particular to such a performance being sandwiched between two teetotal addresses![45].

It was put to Sullivan that even if a right to a performing royalty did exist in non-dramatic songs, it would be extremely difficult to enforce in the remoter parts of England. Sullivan agreed that such collection would be almost impossible when carried out by an author acting as an individual, and he urged very strongly the setting up of a collecting society. But this was not to come for another forty years. The success of the French Society was due to the fact that the early social security organisation in that country was responsible for collecting a local tax from provincial theatres in respect of each performance, so the authors society licensed that organisation to do the collecting on its behalf.

Among the music publishers who automatically assumed that the publisher took the performing right in any assignment of copyright by the author was Henry Littleton of Novellos. When he discovered that there was some doubt about the matter, he had the wording of his forms of assignment altered to ensure that the performing right passed to the publisher[46]. He did not favour the author enjoying a right to prevent the performance of his works for he felt that if this were exercised indiscriminately, it would stop the sale of sheet music, which in his view derived its publicity from performances. By *s.22 Literary Copyright Act 1842* it is provided that no assignment of copyright in any dramatic or literary work shall be taken to convey the performing right in the same work, unless by an entry at Stationers Hall express reference were made to such an intention.

But the point of greatest concern to the publishers was Thomas Wall.

---

45 On the absence of an effective droit moral in the U.K., see McFarlane, "Performing Right", May 1971, p.26.
46 Copyright Commission 1875/6, Minutes of Evidence, p.118.

5

Thomas Wall and copyright legislation prior to 1914

Almost all the witnesses giving evidence to the Copyright Commission of 1875/6 who were concerned with the music industry spoke with disfavour of the practices which had been begun by Thomas Wall at some uncertain date in the years immediately prior to 1875. It was he who had conceived the idea of exploiting the fixed penalty of £2 for unauthorised performances laid down in the *Dramatic Copyright Act 1833* and extended to musical works by the *Literary Copyright Act 1842*, by acting on behalf of the owners of copyright in various musical works to extract large sums of money by way of penalty from unsuspecting music users.

There was no collecting society at that time for musical works, but what set Wall apart from a legitimate society was that, whereas the modern collecting society attempts to publicise its activities, and to induce music users to enter into contractual relations with it on comparatively modest terms, Wall operated after the event and exacted the full penalty, not as a deterrent, but as a ripe fruit to be plucked. But these were the techniques of the common informer, and from their ranks Wall had almost certainly sprung [1]. Like them, his schemes were best served by secrecy, for he stood to gain a greater sum if a performer, unaware of the situation, failed to clear the performing rights and gave a large number of performances. Wall would subsequently claim and, backed by the force of the law, recover £2 for each performance. Because there was so much uncertainty about the right at that time, he was able to flourish; his activities came close to a form of extortion within the framework of the law as it then stood, and eventually legislation had to be passed to curb him, based largely on the evidence taken by the 1875/6 Copyright Commission.

Thus John Boosey described his activities [2]. He stated that an agent had recently started up, who was employed by individuals who had bought out the rights of dead authors, although apparently all the principal living composers of the day had been canvassed by Wall, and

---

1 See Chapter 4 ante.
2 Copyright Commission 1875/6,Minutes of Evidence,p.101.

had not cared to engage him. They took the view that they had composed music in order that it should be performed, and did not care that a dead hand should be placed on those performances. At first Wall's two main clients were a lady who had bought the rights in Wallace's works from his son, and another lady, Mrs. Bodda, who had bought the rights in the works of a composer named Burns. Their employment of Wall caused some stir in the music world, particularly as Mrs. Bodda seemed prepared to press home her claim against those most deserving of consideration. Although he had only begun with a few clients, Wall had formed an organisation with the grandiose title of "The Authors, Composers and Artists Copyright and Performing Right Protective Office", and travelled all over the country in pursuit of persons singing works he controlled. Boosey undoubtedly thought that the shortest way of dealing with the situation would be to abolish the statutory provision altogether, so that there would be no £2 fee, but he was of course opposed to the performing right in any event. He was even more opposed to the rights of deceased authors and composers being purchased for a trifle, and then improperly exercised.

Thomas Chappell had more practical experience of Wall, and has left a fair account of his operations in the Commission's Minutes of Evidence [3]. He spoke bitterly of those people who had bought out deceased authors' rights and then employed Wall, and particularly he resented Mrs. Bodda. Of others he was more tolerant, for as they were not very active in the music world, he thought that no doubt they were very glad to accept £2 from any source available.

It appeared that Wall quite often tried to exact a royalty where no right existed. In one case a famous performer had been about to sing a popular song, when Wall demanded a royalty. Chappell told the performer to ignore him, as Chappell himself claimed to own the right, and he warned Wall not to pursue the matter. This was because of Chappell's practice of buying the performing right from the composer at the same time as he took the publishing right. But other famous publishers, such as Boosey, were not so astute.

Chappell spoke of certain cases which had come to his attention. In one of them a theatrical producer called Bancroft used some eight bars of a song by Wallace as interlude music. The assignee of the rights in Wallace's works had engaged Wall as his agent, and Wall having discovered that the work was being used in the production, gave no notice to the producer, but allowed it to continue, hoping for a long run. In fact

3 Copyright Commission 1875/6,Minutes of Evidence,p.106.

the production was a failure and the show closed after only 20 nights, but nevertheless Wall pressed a claim of £40 in respect of the run, at £2 per performance for eight bars of band music.

He also knew of a publisher who had bought the rights in a popular work by the name of "Tommy make room for your uncle". An agent, probably Wall, approached him and proposed that as the song would be used that Christmas in all the pantomimes, he should ignore the performance at the time, and engage the agent to recover some £500 or £600 when the season was finished. The publisher would have nothing to do with it, and sent the agent packing, as Chappell had done when the same agent had canvassed him. He was unable to tell the Commission precisely how much the agent charged for his services, but he thought it was probably half. Chappell was firmly of the view that the performing right in musical works was intended for operatic works, and that the extension to non-dramatic musical works was something which the legislature had never intended. As exacted by Wall, he considered the statutory sum of £2 a penalty and not a fee.

£2 he agreed would not be a large sum in the case of a big London theatre, but he argued that there were other cases equally affected by Wall. He cited the instance of a benevolent society promoting a small entertainment to raise funds for which a penny admission was charged. Numerous singers had been obliged to settle with Wall, who, when he was dealing with an infringing duet, insisted on £2 from each, and where he came upon a quartette or chorus which had given an unauthorised performance, he took £2 from each member of the group. He agreed with Sullivan[4], when he considered that if a chorus of 50 sang at the Albert Hall, Wall might on this basis be able to obtain a total of £100 from them.

Sullivan has described "this very great source of trouble from certain parties exacting penalties all over the country"[5]. He told the Commission that he had recently been directing certain musical entertainments at which works of Balfe and Wallace had been performed, and that at some time a bill for £80 had been sent in by Wall's agency. Sullivan had simply put it in a pigeon-hole and ignored it.

The Reverend John Bennett had assisted in the organisation of an entertainment to raise funds for the Coggleshall Cricket Club, the programme for which had consisted of music, reading and recitation. A Mrs. Eve of Braintree had sung "Sweet Spirit Hear My Prayer", the

4 See Chapter 4 ante.
5 Copyright Commission 1875/6,Minutes of Evidence,p.113.

performing right in which was owned by a member of the Bodda family, clients of Wall. In due course Mrs. Eve had received a bill for the sum of £2 from Wall, and although she had received legal advice that she might resist the claim, she paid it in order to save unpleasantness [6].

Bennett told the Commission that he had heard that in consequence of Wall's activities, some publishers had a great many sheet copies of songs on their hands which they could not sell. Presumably the public read of a successful action being brought by Wall in respect of a particular song, and refrained from buying it for fear of action being taken against themselves, misunderstanding the difference between a public and private performance.

An intending performer asked Wall if a particular work was controlled by his society, according to Bennett, the enquirer not wishing to infringe. Wall told him that he would not answer unless he subscribed 21 guineas to Wall's society [7]. Bennett himself had visited the publishing house of Novellos, and had been told that he could sing "anything of ours." To clarify the point he had replied "Let me clearly understand you; shall I not be subject to proceedings being taken against me by Mr. Wall for singing any single song that you publish?" The answer given by Novellos was "I think we cannot quite say that; there are some of the songs in which we do not possess the right of performance." Bennett had asked the publishers if they were able to indicate which songs these were, but they were unable to do so. The confusion over who actually owned the performing right in musical works, the copyright in which had been assigned, was yet another reason for the paucity of attempts to exercise it.

A further effect of Wall's activities was a general reluctance among amateurs to give vocal performance in case they should be dunned by his organisation. Bennet had come across instances of this. Ladies in particular feared proceedings being taken against them, which at the least would lay them open to a disagreeable correspondence, and in any case they were uncertain to whom they should apply for permission to perform. Bennet had approached certain ladies to give a similar performance to that which had been given at Braintree, but when they heard of Wall's action after that performance, they said that they would rather

---

6 Copyright Commission 1875/6,Minutes of Evidence,p.115.
7 A modern performing right organisation simply could not give this information, because of the number of works involved throughout the world. To guard against any difficulty of this nature they issue a blanket licence entitling the holder to perform all works in the repertoire of that society and its affiliates.

not sing under any circumstances, even though Bennett undertook to pay any fine which was inflicted.

Wall's pursuit of innocent performers was soon to be brought to an end by statute, largely as a result of the evidence taken by the Commission. The Earl of Devon had sat as a Commissioner on 24th January 1877, and he was able to read to his colleagues a letter issued by Wall's organisation which must have been damning in its effect [8]. An evening gathering had taken place in the little country town of Somerton for the benefit of a local charity and a young lady, the sister of a clergyman in the immediate neighbourhood, had sung a particular song in order to enhance the entertainment and swell the sum received for charity. A few days later she received a letter to the following effect:

"Madam. Re (libretto of) Opera "The Brides of Venice." As for and on behalf of and under a power of attorney from F. H. Bodda Esq., the registered proprietor of the sole liberty of representing, or performing, or causing or permitting to be represented or performed the above, or any part thereof, I hereby claim immediate payment by you unto me of the sum of £2, the amount of statutory penalty incurred by you by having performed, or caused, or permitted to be performed a certain part of the same (to wit) the song entitled "By the Sad Sea Waves" at the Lecture Hall, Somerton on August 14th last, without the consent in writing first had and obtained of the aforesaid proprietor of such said sole libretto (contrary to and against the statutory provisions in that behalf contained.) Unless the above-mentioned amount be paid unto me on or before Wednesday next, the 6th instant, the matter will be placed without further notice in the hands of the solicitors, with instructions to issue legal process against you in respect thereof."

In the light of the opinions expressed in front of the Commission, which led directly to the passing of the *Copyright (Musical Compositions) Act 1882*, an Act which came into force on 10th August 1882, and which was expressed to be to protect the public from vexatious proceedings for the recovery of penalties for the unauthorised performance of musical compositions, it is surprising that the only reported case, decided in the same year of 1882, contained no mention of the Bill then before Parliament, nor when the case went on appeal the next year was there any reference to the Act. Still more surprising is it that only passing reference was made to the criticism voiced of Wall's techniques, though Parliament was prepared to brand his activities as vexatious.

---

8 Copyright Commission 1875/6,Minutes of Evidence,p.194.

The two cases appear in one report, as *Wall v. Taylor* and *Wall v. Martin*[9], and a reader of the evidence of the Copyright Commission has the clear impression that the reports of the cases do not give full flavour of the proceedings. The first refers shortly to a jury trial at first instance in which Wall as assignee of the performing rights had sued for infringement under the *Dramatic Copyright Act 1833* and the *Literary Copyright Act 1842* in respect of the performance of "Will of the Wisp" at Bolingbroke Hall, Clapham Junction, and the Central School Room, Over Darwen, Lancashire. The claim was in each action for 40/- damages or "the full amount of the benefit and advantage arising from such representation or the injury or loss sustained by the plaintiff therefrom, whichever shall be the greater damages." The defendants simply submitted that the song was not dramatic, nor were the places where it was performed places of dramatic entertainment within the meaning of the Act. Wall's counsel argued that it was enough that a musical composition should be performed at a place of public entertainment, and that it need not be a place of dramatic entertainment, so long as admission was paid for. The jury found for the plaintiff in each case, but significantly only awarded 1/- damages, and the judge at first instance ordered the successful plaintiff to pay the defendants' costs, which at least indicated what he thought about the merits of the case.

Wall's counsel sought and obtained a new trial on the ground that the judge had misdirected the jury, by leaving to them the question of whether the musical composition was a dramatic piece within the meaning of the Act, also the question of whether the rooms of performance were places of dramatic entertainment; a further misdirection, he contended, was to tell the jury that there was evidence on which they might find in the negative on both these points, and in particular by telling them that if they found for the plaintiff, but that the work had been performed at a place other than a place of dramatic entertainment, the damages might be as small as they pleased, and not the automatic penalty of £2.

Much argument took place before Field and Cave Jj. in the Queen's Bench Division on the question which had been avoided in *Russell v. Smith*[10] of whether the performing right in a musical work extended to all public performances, or simply those in a place of dramatic entertain-

---

9 (1881) 9 Q.B.D. 727.
10 (1848) 12 Q.B.D. 217.

ment. The judgement of Cave J.[11] is firm on the matter. "No sensible reason was, or as it seems to us could be given why the right of performing a musical composition should be so limited (to a performing right in places of dramatic entertainment) and it is to us quite impossible to conceive any ground for a distinction between performing a musical composition at a place of dramatic entertainment or at a place of entertainment of any other kind." They accordingly found the right conferred to be a general right of public performance, and that therefore the plaintiff in each case was entitled to 40/- as of right, with costs to follow the event.

The case went to the Court of Appeal in respect of both defendants[12]. That court found for Wall on the main issue by a majority of two to one, and although the appeal judges felt that they would have preferred more information about the circumstances of the case and Wall's conduct, they knew enough about him to order that although successful on the main issue, he should have the costs neither of the appeal, nor those incurred in the court below.

The main judgement was that of Lord Esher, then Brett M.R.. He considered that singing for one's own gratification or without the intention to amuse someone else would not be within the meaning of the statutes, and even if someone else happened to be in the same room at the time, that would not be caught. It would be so however where the singing was given a dramatic element, or where it was performed with the intention to amuse others, as it was in the cases then under consideration. If the true effect of *S.21 Literary Copyright Act 1842* was that it only gave a performing right in musical works where, by application of *S.2 Dramatic Copyright Act 1833*, they were performed at places of dramatic entertainment, the learned judge observed that the right would be a dead letter, as in ninety-nine cases out of a hundred, the copyright owner would have no effective remedy. The Master of the Rolls considered that if an infringement of the performing right in a musical work were proved, the penalty or damages of 40/- followed automatically. He added some observations on whether *S.21 Literary Copyright Act 1842* did call for a performance to be at a place of dramatic entertainment for any infringement to be liable to a 40/- penalty. It is unfortunate that the meaning of his remarks are obscure, as authority on the point was so sparse at the time. But the standard of the reporting may be at the root of the trouble[13].

11 9 Q.B.D. 731,732.
12 (1883) 11 Q.B.D.102.
13 See Copinger and Skone-James on Copyright, 11th edn.,para.525.

It does look on the whole as though the conclusion which the learned Master of the Rolls was seeking to draw was that the new right in musical compositions did not require performance at a place of dramatic entertainment, and this is undoubtedly what the case headnote says. The Master of the Rolls had learnt enough of Mr. Wall to observe that in his opinion the action ought not to have been brought, either for damages or penalty, and that it was an attempt to make money out of what had not really done the plaintiff any harm.

The report of Lord Justice Bowen's concurring judgement indicates a clear grasp of the concepts involved. *S.1 Dramatic Copyright Act 1833*, he said, gave a new property right in a dramatic performance, while *S.20 Literary Copyright Act 1842* gave a new right of property in a musical composition. Why by linking that to the requirement of performance at a place of dramatic entertainment should there be read into the newer law what was not a condition or limitation of the penalty in the older law, but simply a part of the description or definition of the previous offence? In a dissenting judgement, Lord Justice Cotton found a performance at a place of dramatic entertainment to be a condition precedent to the penalty of 40/-, and commented that in the absence of such penalty, the plaintiff could always sue for his actual damage. This course would scarcely have appealed to Wall[14].

Words are not minced by the Parliamentary draftsman in his preamble to the *Copyright(Musical Compositions) Act 1882*. "Whereas it is expedient to amend the law relating to copyright in musical compositions, and to protect the public from vexatious proceedings for the recovery of penalties for the unauthorised performance of the same."

By Section 1, the owner of the copyright in any musical composition first published after the passage of the Act who wished to retain the performing right was obliged to have printed on the title page of every published copy of that musical work a notice that the performing right was reserved. By Section 2, where the performing right and the publishing right in the same musical work became vested in separate people prior to publication, then if the owner of the performing right wished to retain it, he was obliged prior to publication to give notice to the owner of the publishing right requiring him to print a reservation of the performing

---

14 The judgement of the Court of Appeal was given on 24th April 1883, subsequent to the **Copyright (Musical Compositions) Act 1882**, which had come into force on 10th August 1882. Although no doubt the decision was in respect of an infringement prior to the Act it is odd that nowhere in that report is any reference made to the Act, or its Bill, passage of which had stemmed directly from the criticism of Wall voiced to the Copyright Commission 1875/6.

right on every published copy. If however the performing right and the publishing right became vested in different people after publication, and prior to such separate vesting of the right notice of reservation of the performing right had been printed on the published copies, then if the owner of the performing right wished to continue to keep it, before any further copies were published, he had to serve notice on the owner of the publishing right requiring him to continue to print the reservation of the performing right.

By Section 3, if the owner of the publishing right failed after such due notice to print on every published copy of the musical work the reservation of the performing right in a proper manner, then he became liable to pay the sum of £20 to the owner of the performing right, to be recoverable in any court of competent jurisdiction. This penalty seems a little inadequate when the effect of failure to print the reservation on an entire edition virtually rendered a musical work free of the performing right so long as such "reservation-free" copies were preserved in existence.

Finally Section 4 attempted to give statutory blessing to the view on costs expressed by Brett M. R. in Wall v.Taylor[15]; it was provided that notwithstanding the *Dramatic Copyright Act 1833* in any action for the infringement of the performing right in a musical work where the plaintiff failed to recover more than the statutory penalty of 40/-, the matter of costs was to be in the discretion of the trial judge. This was intended to be the real sting of the statute so far as Wall was concerned, but even so was only in effect a warning, for at common law the question of costs has always been in the discretion of the trial judge.

This legislation did not finally put paid to Wall, and in spite of the Act he continued to pursue music users for a number of years, so that it was necessary to pass the *Copyright (Musical Compositions) 1888*. Although no case involving Wall had been reported in the meantime, he would appear to have been fairly active in the county courts, as the preamble to the new Act stated that it was "expedient to further amend the law relating to copyright in musical compositions and to further protect the public from vexatious proceedings for the recovery of penalties for the unauthorised performance of the same." It seems that Wall was still able to bring actions for the statutory penalty of 40/-, despite the 1882 Act, and that where there were multiple infringements, he was still able to recover substantial sums and risk his costs. In such cases, it appears that Section 4 of the 1882 Act would not apply as a total of more than 40/- had been recovered.

---

15 11Q.B.D. p.108.

Thus *S.1 Copyright (Musical Compositions) Act 1888* provided that despite the provisions of the *Dramatic Copyright Act 1883*, the penalty or damages for unauthorised performance should be in the absolute discretion of the trial judge, and it specifically provided that he might award less than 40/- per performance, or indeed a nominal sum if the justice of the case demanded it. It also laid down that this section was to affect works published before the Act, as well as works published for the first time thereafter. A weakness of the 1882 Act had been that the printed reservation of the right had only applied to works first published after the passage of that Act.

Furthermore, by S.2,*S.4 Copyright (Musical Compositions) Act 1882* was repealed, and it was provided that in all cases costs were to be in the absolute discretion of the trial judge, and not merely those cases where 40/- or less had been recovered. Finally, by *S.4 Copyright (Musical Compositions) Act 1888*, a large class of potential defendants had been taken away from Wall, for this section exempted from liability for infringement any proprietor, tenant, or occupier of any place at which an unauthorised performance took place, unless he both wilfully caused or permitted such unauthorised performance, and knew it to be unauthorised.

So Wall's activities were finally brought to a halt, but his effect on the development of the performing right had been immense. The *Copyright (Musical Compositions) Acts 1882* and *1888* ensured that no copyright society collecting for musical performances could be set up until after their repeal by the *Second Schedule, Copyright Act 1911*, and that the early operations of the Performing Right Society were to be dogged by the hostility engendered by Wall. He more than any other single reason explains the time lag between the commencement of the collection of royalties in their respective countries for French and British composers.

At the same time it must be remembered that while the entitlement to copyrights for creative workers had never been questioned in France since its inception at the end of the eighteenth century, the copyright laws had never taken root in Britain to anything like the same extent. The great Macaulay was a bitter opponent, and attacked the statutory concept in these terms. "The principle of copyright is this. It is a tax on readers for the purpose of giving a bounty to writers. The tax is an exceedingly bad one; it is a tax on one of the most innocent and salutary of human pleasures; and never let us forget that a tax on innocent pleasures is a premium on vicious pleasures"[16]. Writing a century later,

16 Hansard,vol.LVI, 5th February 1841.

Sir Arnold Plant does not find the case for a copyright monopoly entirely made out [17].

Scandals such as that of the Wall exploitation did nothing to strengthen the growth of the feeble sapling, weak in the late nineteenth century both in the U.K. and the United States. At this stage an excessive exposure of malpractices by sharp operators could have caused the abandonment of the whole system, and Wall was not the only opportunist. Thus in relation to the composition of ragtime piano music in America at the same period, an eminent researcher of the subject has written; "Chauvin was a high-ranking improviser and piano virtuoso, but since he could not read or write music, many of his original tunes and syncopations were transcribed by Scott Joplin without any due credit. In this sense, the whole copyright situation as indicated on the covers of the sheet music is somewhat confused and more than a little misleading if taken literally as an indication of the composer in the academic sense of the term. It is almost impossible at this date to decide with any degree of confidence which of the many pieces that bear Joplin's name as arranger or collaborator were actually composed by him, and how many of them were mere transcriptions originally improvised by other men" [18]. Throughout the nineteenth century in Britain, there is the constant impression that the system is on probation, and that the authorities were only barely satisfied eventually that the right owners were sufficiently responsible to be allowed to operate the new right fully.

From Wall to the Performing Right Society

The *Copyright (Musical Compositions) Acts* of *1882* and *1888* were an artificial solution, and one which limited the intention behind the original performing right statutes; Wall had exploited the right to the fullest permissible limit, and was able to do so because the draftsmen of 1833 and 1842 had failed to provide adequate machinery to operate the Acts. The stopgap reforms of 1882 and 1888 simply put an end to the effective operation of the performing right, and composers, who had been the intended beneficiaries, got nothing.

Quite apart from any question of its effect on the music trade in the United Kingdom, the requirement of reservation of the performing right

---

17 e.g. "The Economic Aspects of Copyright in Books", Economica, May 1934, and "The New Commerce in Ideas and Intellectual Property", Stamp Memorial Lecture, 1953.
18 Dr. Bartlett D. Simms, "History and Analysis of Ragtime", Record Changer, October 1945.

N.°1 IN C   N.° 2 IN D♭   N.° 3 IN F

O FLOWER OF ALL THE WORLD

✳ Song ✳

THE WORDS BY

GILBERT PARKER

(FROM THE SEATS OF THE MIGHTY)

The Music by

AMY WOODFORDE-FINDEN.

PRICE 2/= NET

BOOSEY & ℂ

295, REGENT STREET, LONDON, W.

AND

9, EAST SEVENTEENTH STREET, NEW YORK.

8   *A copy of sheet music, 1897, bearing the publisher's disclaimer.*

in the Acts of 1882 and 1888 was to become in breach of Britain's newly assumed international obligations. This was certainly so once the Berlin Revision of the Berne Convention of 1908 had come into operation, Article 4 of which provided that "the enjoyment and exercise of copyright . . . shall not be subject to any formalities." Because of this, by the *Second Schedule, Copyright Act 1911*, the Acts of 1882 and 1888 were specifically repealed.

The antipathy of the music publishers towards the performing right which had been displayed by Chappell and Boosey to the Copyright Commission of 1875/6 continued. They considered the principle element of their trade to be the sale of sheet music, and they were hostile to anything which might conceivably harm that sale. Successful songs of the late nineteenth century frequently sold sheet copies running into hundreds of thousands, and in some cases into millions. For example, at the time of the Boer War the patriotic melody "Soldiers of the Queen" had sold 238,000 copies in 1898 alone. The publishers feared that this harvest would be reduced by wide public performance in respect of which royalties were levied, and accordingly between 1880 and 1912 it was the practice of the major British publishers not to print the reservation on their sheet copies. The exceptions were the French publishers, for the French authors society, SACEM, had established an agency in London after the ratification by Britain of the Berne Convention to collect in respect of performances in Britain of French works, and accordingly they printed the reservation in order to be able to exercise the right [19].

The British publishers went further than simply failing to print the reservation, for they began to print a disclaimer on their sheet copies. Most copies of British sheet music from the 1880's still extant will be found to bear the legend "may be performed in public without fee or licence." As the practice continued well into the twentieth century it proved a serious embarrassment to early efforts to build up the Performing Right Society, and it did not appear to come to a final end much before 1930 [20]. The staff of PRS still meet enquiries from people who have inherited old copies of sheet music bearing the disclaimer.

Even where the reservation was correctly printed on popular sheet music, the composer did not often bear away the fruit of any success. In the first place, the composer did not have access to any machinery for collection or negotiation of royalties in the shape of a properly organised society, and in the second place he had probably assigned the perfor-

---

19 Unpublished records of PRS.
20 The PR Gazette, 1926.

ming right to a publisher without realising its significance. Curiously enough, the best view is that any failure to print the reservation on a published sheet copy prior to 1911 would mean that, at least as far as that edition is concerned, there would still be no Copyright under the *Copyright Act 1956*.

British publishers were undoubtedly aware of the existence and success of the French collecting society, the Societé des Auteurs. Compositeurs et Éditeurs de Musique, which had been set up in Paris in 1851. It was the first society anywhere in the world for the collection of performance royalties in respect of musical works. As with PRS in Britain over 60 years later, SACEM found the struggle to establish its position extremely difficult in the beginning, and it was obliged to resort to the courts on many occasions, when it was usually successful. Gradually it increased in strength, and the royalties collected for distribution to the members grew, although these were small in the early years.

Eventually the stage was reached where SACEM wished to extend its operations outside France, and an agency was set up in Belgium in 1878. A persuasive campaign led by SACEM resulted in the Belgian Parliament passing a law for the protection of literary and artistic property in 1885, which included a performing right. Agencies of the French society thereafter sprang up in a number of countries, including Holland, Switzerland, Spain, Greece, Monaco, Portugal, Egypt, Romania, Syria and Britain, to press for or to take advantage of laws including a performing right.

Foreign composers in countries lacking a national collecting society were often only too glad to allow an agency of the French Society to demonstrate within their own country that collection of these was a practical proposition. But with the passage of time composers in these countries began to form their own national societies which became affiliated to SACEM and replaced the agencies. There is no doubt that it was the example of SACEM which led to the successful establishment of similar societies all over the world. Not only did the French agency in Britain do much to help PRS come into being, but Pierre Sarpy its general manager became the first holder of that post at PRS.

After SACEM, the next national societies in their own right to be set up were Italy (1883), Austria (1897), Spain (1899), and Germany (1903). As in Britain, the first society in the United States was established in 1914 [21].

---

21 See in general McFarlane on Copyright Collecting Societies, Grove's Dictionary of Music and Musicians, (Macmillan) 6th edn.

Soon technical change was to overtake the complacency of the British publishers. A cancer on the legitimate music industry which had grown as the nineteenth century drew to a close had been the sale of pirated copies of sheet music through street hawkers. In many ways very similar to the pirate records which undermine the gramophone industry today, the pirated copies of sheet music were photographed or lithographed very cheaply, and put on sale at a fraction of the original publication cost. The street hawkers were invariably men of straw, and the great difficulty of finding anyone of substance to take responsibility allowed the pirates to flourish.

The *Musical (Summary Proceedings) Copyright Act 1902* was passed in an attempt to stamp out the nuisance, but it merely gave a power to seize and destroy copies which had been pirated. As it created no criminal offence it was of little effect. It was totally inadequate, and in April 1905 the nineteen members of the Music Publishers Association announced that they would accept no more music for publication, nor would they enter into any fresh contracts for payments to singers of new publications. As this meant that their main sources of profit from sales of sheet music and concert promotion would disappear, it was made clear to the Legislature that they had been driven into this position by the lack of effective protection against piracy [22].

This action had a rapid effect, for on 4th August 1906, the *Musical Copyright Act 1906* came into force. It created a criminal offence of printing, reproducing, selling, exposing or offering or possessing for sale any printed copies of sheet music, or possessing any plates for the purpose of making pirate copies. The statute was reinforced by giving the police a right of entry to search premises for pirated copies. Though this had the effect of stamping out the pirate trade, it acted together with rapid technical change to bring to an end the complaisant attitude of the music industry to the performing right.

Edison had invented the phonograph in 1877, but for some twenty years it remained little more than a novelty toy. But wax discs replaced the cylinders in 1895, in 1897 the clock spring motor gave a truer running speed, and in 1905 the double sided disc gave the gramophone record commercial significance. Mass production and trans-Atlantic sales techniques soon made inroads into the publishers' and composers' income from sheet music sales, and both began to think of the performing right as a possible source of income.

---

22 William Boosey, ''Fifty Years of Music'',p.115.

93

The attention of the British music trade was increasingly drawn to the success which the French agency of SACEM in London was enjoying. Fortified by British accession to the Berne Convention in 1886, it was deriving a significant income in collecting for performances in the U.K. of French compositions, while the British composer went unrewarded in his own country [23].

The increase in leisure experienced by all classes in the late nineteenth century must also have led to an increase in the demand for music [24]. Not only was there a large number of amateur musicians of high accomplishment, but also a great increase in the number of professional composers, musicians and teachers. The demand for self-entertainment prior to the gramophone had given employment to a large number of music teachers, and the pupils they produced used large quantities of sheet music.

Prior to the advent of the gramophone the music publishers had also controlled the majority of concert outlets, but by the 1880's these were in decline. Novellos began to lose money on their Albert Hall concerts, and by 1898 Chappells had been forced to end their St.James Hall series. The publishing firms which owned or leased concert halls started to suffer losses, and a decline had set in for the music publishers [25]. So they began to consider that the performing right which they had discounted before the Copyright Commission 1875/6 might in fact be more than just a defence.

Fortunately for British composers, this shift in opinion coincided with a realisation that a review of copyright law was required, both in order to conform with the international requirements of the Berne Convention, and to rationalise the confused jumble of legislation on the subject which then existed. When the *Copyright Act 1911* came into force on 1st July 1912, by its Second Schedule it repealed in their entirety no fewer than 17 statutes relating to the subject of copyright, the earliest of which was the *Engraving Copyright Act 1734*.

The list included the *Dramatic Copyright Act 1833* and the *Literary Copyright Act 1842* and in their place an effective performing right was substituted. *By S.1 Copyright Act 1911*, copyright was to exist in every original literary, dramatic, musical and artistic work, and by S.1(2), copyright was deemed to be infringed by anyone who, without the consent of the owner of the copyright did anything the sole right to do

23 C. F. James, "The Story of the PRS", (1951),p.16.
24 E. D. Mackerness, A Social History of English Music, pp.175/177.
25 Economists Advisory Group, The Economic Value of Music Composition (1972),p.15.

which was vested by the Act in the owner of the copyright. So at last an effective statutory provision had been made in unambiguous terms, and British composers, authors, and publishers were soon to act in unison to take advantage of it.

6

The setting up of the Performing Right Society

Consultations had taken place in 1913 on the feasability of setting up a collecting society in the changed situation following the coming into force of the *Copyright Act 1911*. Guided by the general manager of the London agency of the French society SACEM, who was to become the first general manager of PRS[1], interested parties set in hand the obtaining of a lease on suitable premises, and sufficient funds to begin operations. On 6th March 1914, the Performing Right Society was registered as a limited company. The first general meeting of the new company took place on 1st April 1914, after which effective operation of the performing rights of the original 39 members began.

While this book is an account of the development of the performing right itself, from this point forward a large part of the history must be traced from the development of PRS. This is not to render the rest of the work simply a history of PRS: however the Society was the only organisation in Britain attempting to collect in respect of performing rights on such a vast scale. It fought most of the major battles to establish the principles, and by virtue of its operations became extremely well known. Because of its position it began to be consulted by Government on matters of copyright reform, and its representatives appeared at international conferences on intellectual property from an early date [1a].

The constitution of the Society was that of a company limited by guarantee, the principal objects of which were the licensing of members' rights, and the collection and distribution of royalty receipts accruing in respect of that licensing. The Society only came into being because of the active support of its first publisher members who provided the necessary finance, and at that time it was the practice of

---

1 See Chapter 5 ante.
1a The writer has had the considerable advantage of working in legal offices of the music industry for some years, 3 of them with PRS itself. He has had the great assistance of access to files from early days which are invaluable to this study, but which are usually unpublished, and frequently long forgotten. It follows that sometimes no more formal reference can be given than to ''Unpublished Records''; in many cases all participants at particular meetings are deceased, and the matter can be taken no further than the statement on the file.

publishers to take a full assignment of copyright from the first owners, who were the writers of the works being published. Being uncertain of the prospects of the new Society, these publishers were reluctant to relinquish control of their property in its entirety. They declined to transfer the performing right in their works to the Society, and would only grant it authority to exercise that right on behalf of themselves and their writers. Thus in those early days the members merely granted the Society the sole right to authorise or to forbid the public performance of their works, and the sole right to collect royalties in respect of those performances.

This was to have considerable disadvantages for the infant Society, which could not therefore commence infringement actions in its own name, but was obliged to proceed in the name of the owner or to join him. It was moreover hampered by certain owners who alienated the right by contract with non-members, sometimes agreeing not to enforce it in particular cases; sometimes also certain members made agreements between themselves purporting to vary the Society's rules. Some publishers even made it an express condition of joining that they retained ownership of the performing right, and only granted the Society a licensing authority. It was twenty years before the Society was able to correct this position finally from a situation of strength[2].

The outbreak of the First World War almost immediately after it was opened for business was a considerable set-back to the new Society. It thus had to begin its struggle to set up a system of collection and distribution not only in a community which was at that time basically hostile to the enforcement of the concept, but one in which too strident a campaign by PRS was likely to encounter severe Government disapproval as detracting from the war effort.

Apart from the difficulties caused by the absence of the reservation of the performing right on pre-1912 works, the initial small membership of the Society had the result that only a small proportion of the national musical heritage lay under the Society's control. It was thus of immense advantage to PRS to conclude reciprocal contracts with the corresponding societies which already existed in France, Italy, Germany and Austria. This addition to its repertoire at the outset enabled it to license a far greater range of works than would otherwise have been the case. Moreover, a helpful basis was provided by the contracts already existing between certain British music users and the British agency of the French society. By the reciprocal contract of affiliation the French society

---

2 Unpublished Records of PRS.

ceased to collect in Britain, and the British society acquired the exclusive right to administer the performing right on its behalf for French works. Thus a nucleus of contracting parties existed which was at least attuned to dealing with a collecting society. This vital basis enabled operations to begin, and gradually the repertoire and the operation increased with a growth in membership, and new compositions and publications by existing members.

The technique of loss-leading was also applied, as the Society was so desperate to have at least the principle of its existence recognised. If a music-user were prepared to go as far as to acknowledge the Society's rights by contract, then the Society would enter into agreement on a tariff based on almost any terms, however nominal. It was felt at that time that they could be adjusted upwards to more realistic rates when the Society became more firmly accepted. This acceptance was to take far longer than the founder members of the Society had originally imagined[3].

Not until 1917 was it deemed practicable to authorise the first distribution to members. At that time they numbered 297, and between them they received at that first distribution just over £11,000. It must have seemed to them that the Society was set on a course of continued expansion.

But in 1919, a substantial group of publishers withdrew from PRS, taking with them their associated authors and composers. There were two main reasons, on the one hand, doubts about the value of the Society, and on the other, organised opposition from the performers, in the shape of the Amalgamated Musicians' Union (now the Musicians' Union). These publishers were all firms which had been set up immediately after the war to exploit the new craze for dance music by publishing sheet music for the new works[4]. It is hard to tell why they joined PRS in the first place, as they left en masse almost at once. They believed however that sales of sheet music would continue to provide a sufficient return for the publisher, and that free permission for performance compensated for the loss of performing right royalties by the value of the advertisement acquired. They were not able to maintain this position for long, for the reduction in price of gramophone records and the inception of broadcasting in 1922 exposed this point of view as fallacious, and by 1926 they had been obliged to rejoin the Society in order to obtain compensation for the broadcasting of their material[5].

3 Unpublished Records of the P.R.S.
4 E. D. Mackerness, A Social History of English Music (London 1964) p.251.
5 Economists' Advisory Group,op.cit.p.40.

The Musicians' Union felt that the Society's operations might lessen the opportunities for employment of its members. In particular it objected to the system of blanket licensing adopted by the Society which, the Union argued, meant that the music user was being asked to pay for the right to perform non-copyright music. This was a fallacy, for the Society's royalty was only levied in respect of the works which it controlled. However, the Society had made a serious diplomatic blunder in the previous year, when it had suggested basing its tariffs for music use on the number of musicians employed. This immediate threat to musicians' employment was rapidly dropped, but the hostility remained[6].

Accordingly in 1919 the Musicians' Union threatened to boycott performances of works in the PRS repertoire, and this threat also contributed to the withdrawal of the dissident publishers. The menace caused the Society to initiate legal proceedings against the Union. They are not reported, but PRS obtained an injunction, and although the Union appealed, it abandoned the contest, and withdrew its boycott[7].

The music users who comprised the licensees and whose royalties provided PRS with its income were constantly in opposition. The Society has always attempted to come to arrangements with representative organisations whereby a single tariff could be agreed to cover one entire category of music user, for example the Showmans' Guild, and the Theatrical Managers' Association. Although several such arrangements were made in the early days, many trade organisations tried to defeat the Society by banding together in opposition. Parliamentary lobbying was to have a certain effect, but more direct means of attack were also brought to bear. For example, in about 1919 an organisation called the British Music Union Limited began to operate in an attempt to undermine the Society. It published and advertised a so-called catalogue of "Free Music", which was composed of music which was either out of copyright, or for which the publisher did not assert the performing right. In this enterprise it met with very little success, and as the strength and membership of PRS grew, so the impact of "free music" passed altogether[8].

But in the Society's first years it had to deal with a great number of music users who were outside any organisation or body, but who were

---

6 Report of the Select Committee on the Musical Copyright Bill 1930, questions 787,813/7.
7 Unpublished Records of the PRS.
8 Report of the Select Committee on the Musical Copyright Bill 1930 question 461.

determined to fight the Society at every step. By simply ignoring its requests, they forced the PRS administration to decide at a very early stage that as a matter of policy such people would have to be taken to court on every occasion on which the ignored demands reached a certain stage. So almost from the outset PRS was bringing a number of actions regularly at High Court level in the Chancery Division for infringement of copyright[9].

These infringement actions became a regular feature of the Society's operations, and were quite apart from the actions to decide the scope and effect of the statutory performing right. The latter were tried regularly in the decades following the Society's establishment, and a number of them are reported. They will be dealt with in a separate chapter.

When the Society had been set up in 1914, few of the early publishers considered that the revenue from performing rights would ever form the greater part of their income, but before long they began to take the same view as the noted publisher William Boosey who had observed, "I was gradually becoming aware that, probably, eventually a composer's performing rights might be even more valuable than his publishing rights"[10]. The piracy of sheet music was discussed in Chapter 5 ante; no doubt the piracy began the psychological process, but the rapid change which had overtaken the music industry in the gramophone section was to bite deep into the sheet music market.

Converted from a novelty into a practical commercial proposition[11], it remained for some time a high cost product, copies of Patti's records of "Home Sweet Home" costing £1 each in 1906. But the application of American techniques of marketing and mass-production altered the situation very quickly, and the price of both gramophones and their records came into direct opposition with sheet music[12]. The British composers and publishers turned the new industry to their own advantage in part by securing the mechanical right by *S.19 Copyright Act 1911*, while American right owners obtained a similar right by *S.1 U.S.Code,Title*

---

9 For about fifty years a high annual level of writs was maintained, though from about 1970 the number of infringement actions began to decrease sharply. Now the annual figure is generally below 30, and only rarely is a defence entered. The reason for this decrease is not yet clear, but it may be due to there remaining only a small number of unlicensed music users, coupled with a more general acceptance of PRS by the community at large.
10 Copyright Royalty (Mechanical Musical Instruments) Inquiry 1928, Minutes of evidence,p.175.
11 See Chapter 5 ante.
12 Economists Advisory Group,op.cit.,p.12.

17,1909. Increasingly the publishers were to turn to the exploitation of the new performing right to make up the shortfall in their income, and this dependence on the performing right continued to grow after the introduction of broadcasting in 1922, which drew heavily on gramophone records to make up its material.

7
The First PRS Cases

Atkin J. tried the first infringement action brought by the Society, which was heard in the King's Bench Division on 10th April 1918. It is reported as *Performing Right Society v. Thompson*[1] The defence did not advance the sophistication of argument which was to be put forward by infringers in following cases, and as reported displayed little familiarity with the concepts at issue. As pleaded, the defence amounted to no more than that the business carried on by the plaintiffs was that of "breedbates" and "trafficking in litigation." This provoked the following reported exchange.

"His Lordship: What is meant by the word "breedbates"? Mr. Thomas: It is a good Shakespearian expression, My Lord. "No telltale nor no breed-bate" - a provoker of strife."

The claim was for the infringement of the performing right in the songs "If you were the only girl in the world" and "Keep The Home Fires Burning", by the pianist employed by the proprietor of the Cinema Royale in Epsom. The defendant in evidence said that he had instructed his pianists to avoid playing copyright pieces, a point which was to be taken up in later and better reported cases, and the pianist in question said that she had been instructed to extemporise and to avoid popular songs. She denied that she had ever played "Keep The Home Fires Burning", that she had ever seen the music of that song, or that she had ever heard it played through. Observed His Lordship, "They must be very fortunate people down at Epsom."

The judge held that as the Society had been formed to protect the rights of authors, then if necessary resort might be had to litigation. The objects of the Society were in every way genuine and legitimate, and were carried out by genuine and legitimate methods. It had been argued that the rules under which the Society operated brought it within the law then obtaining against maintenance and champerty.

By its rules PRS pooled all royalty income and any damages recovered as a result of litigation, and divided the sum among the members after deduction of any administrative expenses. The defendants had argued that this was champertous and void, but it was held to be a bona fide

---

1 (1918) 34 T.L.R.351.

business arrangement between the Society and its members. The Society had a real and bona fide interest in the result of the litigation, and the provision for the division of damages was merely subsidiary to the real transaction. An injunction was granted against the defendant and astonishingly the sum of £4 was awarded as damages, the exact amount which would have been due under the *Literary Copyright Act 1842* for the infringement of two works.

The next reported case was that of *Performing Right Society v. Edinburgh Magistrates*[2], in which a much more serious defence was raised before the Scottish courts. *S.5 Trade Union Act 1871* enacted that "the Companies Acts 1862 and 1867 shall not apply to any trade union, and the registration of any trade union under the said acts shall be void." *S.16 Trade Union Act Amendment Act 1876* provided that "The term "trade union" means any combination . . . for imposing restrictive conditions on the conduct of any trade or business, whether such combination would or would not, if the principal Act (of 1871) had not been passed, have been deemed to have been an unlawful combination by reason of some one or more of its purposes being in restraint of trade."

The defendants pleaded that the plaintiff company was an association formed to carry on a business in restraint of trade, and was endeavouring to obtain control of and to create a monopoly in popular light music, inter alia. If the decision had rested on the situation under the 1876 Act, the Society would have been in some difficulty, as Lord Hunter implied in his opinion at first instance[3]. It will be recalled that in about 1875 the Dramatic Authors Society had been refused permission to both have a charter of incorporation and to sue in its own name as a friendly society as it appeared to the Treasury that its purposes were sufficiently in restraint of trade to render it capable of registration under the trade union legislation of 1871 and 1876. If then the Performing Right Society was held to be liable to registration as a trade union, its registration as a company would be void, and it would have had no title to sue as a company.

Fortunately for PRS however, *S.1(2) Trade Union Act 1913* had since enacted, "For purposes of this Act, the expression "Statutory objects" means the objects mentioned in section sixteen of the Trade Union Amendment Act 1876, namely the registration of the relations between workmen and masters, or between workmen and workmen, or between masters and masters, or the imposing of restrictive conditions

---

2 1922 S.C.165.
3 1922 S.C. @169.

on the conduct of any trade or business, and also the provision of benefits to members." S.2(1) had enacted "The expression "trade union" for the purpose of the Trade Union Acts 1871 to 1906, and this Act, means any combination, whether temporary or permanent, the principal objects of which are under its constitution statutory objects."

As Lord Hunter observed at first instance, this considerably curtailed the scope of the 1871 and 1876 Acts. The performing right, he said, was a peculiar piece of property, unlike ordinary subjects of manufacture which may be produced by any commercial man, where the public had an interest that the prices should be regulated by fair competition in the open market, and not by a combination of manufacturers who maintained prices at an artificial level. The performing right in his view was a privilege or monopoly right conferred by statute to encourage invention, and thereby to benefit the public by addition to its stock of original works.

This approach has much to commend it to any copyright collecting society, for a frank acceptance that the performing right is a statutory monopoly right is more likely to forestall criticism based on monopolistic grounds than any pretence that copyright is somehow an inherent property right with roots in legal philosophy.

Not all commentators on the subject share this view, least of all on the Continent. Thus Dr. Dock states: "In the Anglo-Saxon countries, copyright has its roots in the old law and in the common-law connected with the publishing privileges of former times. There copyright consists of a monopoly of exploitation and has the appearance of an artificial creation. This pragmatic approach, both utilitarian and social, is not that adopted by the Latin countries "[4].

It is perhaps easier to argue that the rights of creators of artistic works are in some way entitled to natural rights which are above mere human legislation. It is undoubtedly difficult in the case of a patent right or a trademark. Professor Darenberg in a comparative study of the laws of unfair competition draws attention to the difference of approach between the European and the common law countries[5]. He suggests that the piece-meal approach to a law of unfair competition both in the United States and in Britain, and by implication to the whole field of intangible rights, should be contrasted with the position in France. There immediately after the Revolution trade guilds and associations were prohibited by a Statute of May 1791. The law against unfair comp-

---

4 Marie-Claude Dock,Étude sur le Droit d'Auteur,(1963),p.167.
5 4 American Journal of Comparative Law,p.1.

etition is so firmly entrenched in the Code that in some cases an aggrieved plaintiff may prefer to seek his remedy there rather than to sue specifically under patent or copyright law.

On appeal in the same report the approach of Lord Hunter was upheld and applied by Lord Clyde the Lord President, and by Lord Mackenzie, Lord Skerrington concurring. The text in the *Trade Union Act 1913* was whether one of the principal objects of a company was to impose restrictive conditions on a trade or business. The members agreed to contribute their performing rights to a joint venture, which they endowed with the necessary powers, because they considered that it could exploit and protect those rights better than they could do by themselves as individuals. These objects were not in restraint of trade, they were in support and prosecution of it.

This favourable judgement came at a crucial time for the young society, for a defeat in an early reported case might have set back its operations by years. The argument that an organisation operating a monopoly right to collect funds, particularly when it imposed licences and employed a system of collectors, could well be taken to be operating in restraint of trade on cursory examination [6].

A case in England on very similar facts was proceeding through trial at first instance and on appeal on a time scale slightly behind that of the Edinburgh Magistrates Case. This was the *Performing Right Society v. London Theatre of Varieties*[7]. In an action by the Society for the infringement of their copyright by the performance of "A Devonshire Wedding" and "Love in Lilac Time", the defendants raised the plea that the plaintiff society was a trade union, and therefore unable to sue, also that as assignees it could not sue without joining the assignors as co-plaintiffs. At first instance, Branson J. decided both points in favour of PRS, granting the Society a perpetual injunction, and assessing damages in the familiar sum of 40/-. On appeal this decision was upheld, Bankes L. J. recalling that although the original definition of a trade union in the 1871 Act had been replaced by that of the 1876 Act, the test to be applied since 1913 was whether the principal objects of any organisation were in restraint of trade. Although the Society was undoubtedly a combination, its principal objects were not within the statutory definition. It followed that PRS was not a trade union, and accordingly its right to sue as a corporation registered under the Companies Acts was unimpaired.

---

6 As late as 1973 PRS had to appeal against a misunderstanding of the right by the Court of Session. See **PRS V.Rangers Supporters Clubs 1973 SLT 198**, to be discussed later.
7 [1922] 2K.B.433 in the Court of Appeal.

The second point was less easily disposed of. Bankes L. J. decided that an equitable assignee of copyright could not sue in his own name for infringement of copyright unless there were some provision in the *Copyright Act 1911* to the contrary. S.6 in dealing with the ownership of copyright gave the civil remedies for infringement to the copyright owner, while S.5 gave the copyright owner the right to assign. The position of the Society was that of an equitable assignee, which could not maintain the present action without joining the legal owners of the copyright to the action. As at the time of taking the assignment of the copyright from the publishers in 1914, including all the performing rights which they then possessed or should thereafter acquire, the Society was a mere equitable assignee. The works in question were specifically assigned by the composers to the publishers after they had been written in about 1919 or 1920, but clearly it would have been impracticable for the Society to take a fresh legal assignment in respect of each work as it was written, for at the time of that action it controlled over one million titles[8]. The appeal was accordingly allowed on that point, with the provision that the Society should be given the opportunity to amend by joining the legal owners of the copyright as parties.

The Society declined to join the legal owners, but appealed to the Lords on the point of its right to sue in its own name[9]. The claim for damages was abandoned, and the main argument in the case was concentrated on the point which the Society had lost in the Court of Appeal, although some slight attention was directed to the trade union point. Their Lordships did not disagree with the lower court on that issue, but unfortunately for the Society they were firmly against it on the question of assignment.

Viscount Cave agreed that an equitable owner could commence proceedings alone and obtain an interim injunction, but considered that where a party had only an equitable right to the thing demanded, the person having the legal right to demand it must in due course be made a party. Accordingly he held that the Society was unable to obtain the injunction it sought. Viscount Finlay suggested that the remedy for PRS might be to take a special assignment conveying the legal interest in respect of any work about to become the subject of litigation, or to join the legal owner as a plaintiff, or if he refused, to add him as a defendant.

This decision was very serious for the Society, for against the solution offered by Viscount Finlay was the objection that it was not always

---

8 At the present time the number is many times greater, and it is virtually impossible to state precisely how many works are controlled at any given time.
9 [1924] A.C.1.

possible to trace the legal owner with ease. If an individual, he might always have emigrated, if a corporation, it might have gone into liquidation, or be in the course of being taken over. As a result, although its opponents were not generally aware of the fact in those early days, PRS was considerably restricted in the infringement cases which it brought; it only took action where the chain of title was clear, and had been carefully researched. Although under reciprocal contracts the Society controlled in the U.K. works written by composers abroad, until the 1956 Act in practice it never brought infringement actions in respect of their works, and thereafter only in exceptional cases, due to the problems of effectively proving assignments [10].

At an early date the question of authorisation of performances was ventilated. In the *Performing Right Society v. Mitchell & Booker* [11], the defendants who occupied a dance-hall had engaged a band under contract, one of the terms of which was that the band should not infringe any copyright or other proprietary right of third parties. The defendants also caused to be displayed on the wall of the dance-hall a prominent notice that "only such music as may be played without fee or licence is allowed to be played at this hall." The defendants had not taken out the Society's licence, and it was admitted that on one occasion the band played tunes the performing right in which was controlled by the Society, although the defendant proprietors were unaware that the infringement had taken place, and had by contract and disclaimer appeared to have done as much as possible to prevent an infringing performance. In the early nineteen twenties there was still a sufficiently large amount of popular music outside the PRS control to enable a band to avoid infringing by using this wide repertoire of non-copyright works. When challenged, the band leader had replied that he was unaware that the works were under the control of the Society, adding that he did not know what works were controlled by it, and that as the defendants his employers had not taken out its licence, he had found it hard to establish what was and was not included in its repertoire.

McCardie J. held that the band had been acting in the course of its employment, despite the fact that the defendants were unaware of the infringement, and had taken steps to prevent it. Accordingly an injunction was granted.

A similar case was in progress through the courts at the same period.

---

10 By **S.37(1)Copyright Act 1956** provision is made for assignment by a prospective owner of copyright so that when a future work comes into existence, the assignee acquires the legal title at once, and obtains all the remedies open to a copyright owner.
11 [1924] 1 K.B.762.

In *Performing Right Society v. Ciryl Theatrical Syndicate Ltd.*[12], the defendant company was the lessee of a theatre, and a second defendant was that company's director, the company by the managing director as its agent engaging an orchestra. The second defendant was responsible for the production of the play, but the company was responsible for the front of the curtain, including the engagement of the orchestra. The second defendant as agent of the first defendant had told the band leader that no copyrights were to be infringed. At first instance Rowlatt J. had held that both the company and its managing director had authorised infringing performances of works the performing rights in which were controlled by PRS, and both were accordingly held liable, although neither defendant had been aware of the performances.

The second defendant appealed, and the hearing in the Court of Appeal is also reported[13]. Bankes L. J. agreed that indifference as to whether or not a particular work was performed might reach a degree from which positive authorisation could be inferred, each case turning on its own facts. In the present case it appeared that the second defendant had been abroad at the time of the infringements, and also when the Society had first written to him complaining about them. Accordingly, as the band were neither the servants nor the agent of the managing director, he was not liable for their infringing performances.

Scrutton L. J. concurred, and his views are important, as he appeared in most of the leading copyright cases in the years prior to his appointment to the Bench, while his textbook, when current in the late nineteenth century had at least as much weight as the then current editions of its contemporary Copinger. As the managing director had been on the Continent, he had known nothing of these performances. It could not be said that he had authorised a performance, because he had not caused it, the performers being neither his servants nor his agents, but on the contrary the servants or agents of the company, which was itself the principal of the managing director. Although in Mitchell & Booker it had been felt that the Ciryl case did not apply because of the absence of a master and servant relationship between the musicians and the managing director, the facts are otherwise very similar, and in Mitchell & Booker the defendants could hardly have gone to greater lengths to prevent an unauthorised performance.

Nevertheless there was a direct finding by McCardie J. that the band had there been employed under a contract of service. The dance-hall

12 [1923] 2 K.B.147.
13 [1924] 1 K.B.1.

proprietors enjoyed "the right of continuous, dominant and detailed control on every point, including the nature of the music to be played." This case is said by several authorities to have been an application of the principle of vicarious liability in the law of torts, for as copyright is a statutory chose in action, a breach thereof is a tort. According to Professor Atiyah, McCardie J. was using the control test of vicarious liability, whereby had the master taken a little care in supervising the servant's performance of the task, he might have secured the performance of the work without the injury. Atiyah concedes that the conditions of modern industrial society render any attribution of fault to the master the purest fiction, but the learned judge did not feel inhibited by any such consideration, for he referred firmly to the prohibition in the employees' contract and the prominence of the disclaimer, concluding that despite this it did not absolve the defendants from the acts of their employees in the course of their employment [14].

The Ciryl case has to be reconciled with this finding by the fact that it was only the second defendant, the director, who appealed, and that therefore the finding of liability against the first defendant, the company, remained undisturbed. Ciryl's case is cited as authority for the proposition that the directors of a limited company cannot be held liable for the torts of a servant of the company, unless they ordered and procured the acts to be done, merely by virtue of their position as directors. If there are facts from which it may be inferred that the relationship of principal and agent has been established between the directors and the company, they may be liable, but the mere fact that they are the sole directors and shareholders is not sufficient [15].

14 Atiyah, "Vicarious Liability in the Law of Torts." p.41.
15 Clerk and Lindsell on Torts, 13th edn., para.174.

8
Consolidation of the Society's early gains

By 1921 the Society's business had expanded sufficiently to allow it to move to newer and larger premises, and an immense step forward was taken in 1923 when the first licence was issued to the infant B.B.C. (between 1922 and 1926 known as the British Broadcasting Company.) This early acceptance of the concept of the performing right by the new medium of broadcasting made the survival of PRS much more likely; had radio in Britain developed along commercial lines this acceptance would probably not have been so readily achieved.

The copyright owners had little alternative however. "In November 1923, for example, London was broadcasting on an average each day 3 hours and 25 minutes of music to 2 hours and 5 minutes of everything else"[1]. The rapid growth in licence numbers threw up the problem for the members of the Society in even sharper terms. 595,496 licence holders in 1923 had grown to 2,178,259 only three years later.[2]

While the Society's domestic repertoire grew at an extremely satisfactory rate, an expansion in the number of contracts of affiliation with overseas collecting societies swelled the total of works which PRS was able to offer in its licence. During the early twenties the Society entered into relationships with its sister organisations in Czechoslovakia, Denmark, Hungary, Poland, Spain, Sweden and the U.S.A., together with special agencies operating in Belgium and Holland.

These two last agencies were operated in those days by SACEM, the French society; PRS quickly began to imitate this well-tried policy of establishing agencies in overseas territories where no national organisation existed. This was after all how the French society had operated since the late nineteenth century in the U.K. prior to establishment of PRS[3]. Local authors were encouraged to join PRS until their local societies grew into independent agencies in their own right. The Society was particularly fortunate in being able to push its links out into the Dominions and Colonies of those days. So much had the network grown,

---

1 Professor A. Briggs, The History of Broadcasting in the U.K. vol.1,p.275.
2 Professor A. Briggs, ibid,p.18.
3 See Chapter 5 ante.

that at the Society's annual dinner of 1924, the President was able to forecast a time when the composers' income from performing rights would exceed that of sheet music[4]. The inroads made by gramophone records into sales of sheet music editions was to ensure that this shift in emphasis was not long delayed.

The contracts of affiliation called for a vast exchange of information between the linked societies, and rules were drawn up by contract and by their international association (CISAC) to regulate the situation. Although each national society was free to adopt whatever system it chose for its own distribution of domestic revenues, when dealing with foreign societies they could not by the application of their own distribution plans favour their own members. Although driven no doubt by self-interest, the international system of copyright collecting societies has provided a remarkable example of co-operation across national frontiers. The effect is not that of an international company, but of linked national monopolies[5,6,7].

The internal system of collection and distribution of revenue is complex, and has followed much the same pattern since the Society's early days. It is even now very close to the system described to the Copyright Commission 1875/6 by the Secretary of the Dramatic Authors Society[8]. It was clearly impossible when using a system of blanket licences to establish precisely which performances were attributable to each composer member. Thus by a term of each licence issued by the Society for both live performances and broadcasts, regular returns of the music performed were required to be made by the licensee. Although only a small number of these returns were in fact sent in, an analysis was conducted which showed how often each work was performed. To this a points system was applied, a test based on length of work, type of performance, and also the character of the work. The rarer performances of classical works were also heavily subsidised by the ephemeral popular performances. This is still the case[9].

By the 1920's the cinema had emerged from its magic lantern state, and began to attract large audiences. At first it affected the musical world only by its use of live music, generally on piano, to accompany silent films, as was the case in the Society's first action, *Performing*

---

4 Unpublished records of PRS.
5 For examination of the monopoly situation, see Chapter 12 post..
6 For the foundation of CISAC, see Chapter 11 post.. See also:
7 Unpublished records of PRS.
8 See Chapter 4 ante.
9 McFarlane, copyright Collecting Societies, Grove's Dictionary of Music and Musicians, 6th edn., (Macmillan).

Right Society Ltd.v.Thompson[10]. But by 1927, sound had been synchronised with the images on the screen, and with this technical breakthrough, the visit to the cinema became "the essential social habit of the age "[11]. The silent films had actually provided a new outlet for the composer, specialising in "photo-play" music to match the emotions being acted out on the screen in silence[12]. Soon the distinctive term "background music" came into vogue, to distinguish it from the "feature music", which the actors are actually supposed to hear.

Certainly the cinema provided much employment for musicians, though even before the advent of sound films, the use of special arrangements for whole cinema circuits led to a degree of cutback on music specially composed for silent film audiences. The "talkies" themselves threw the situation out of balance, for on the one hand a vast field of employment was withdrawn from the musician working in the cinema, while on the other the composer specialising in film music was to become among the most highly paid category of PRS member. A single performance synchronised on sound track was opened up to an audience of hundreds of millions on the international circuits. Arthur Bliss, Benjamin Britten and William Walton were among the most eminent composers of the day attracted to the new medium. But the rise of the cinema was perhaps the final nail in the coffin of self-entertainment in the home, those performances the summit of which had been attained in the Victorian drawing-room, and which had for so long sustained the sales of sheet music.

Radio itself provided in Britain an alternative source of employment for musicians. Although gramophone records had been employed in broadcasting as early as 1922, the BBC did not then use them as a low-cost alternative to live performers. Rather by the promotion of the BBC Orchestras, with the emphasis on quality and education, the BBC showed itself to be a substantial patron of serious music, and the musicians and composers connected with it[13].

But music programmes on radio provided a temptation for publishers and composers to pay dance band leaders for the promotion of their works during broadcasts. Even in the nineteenth century there had been a tradition of costing by publishers for the expenses of promoting a new song, which continued into the first decades of this century. These costs involved engagements of singers, concert promotion, newspaper adver-

10 (1918) 34 T.L.R.351.
11 A. J. P. Taylor, English History 1914-1945,p.392.
12 Economists Advisory Group,op.cit., p.26.
13 Economists Advisory Group,op.cit.,p.32.

tising, and maintaining travellers throughout the country [14]. One publisher claimed to be spending £1000 per week during the summer of 1928 "plugging his firm's publications through dance and concert bands in the main seaside resorts". His firm had spent on a song which brought in only £1085 no less than £4000 on publicity for it. This had included sending lantern slides and words of the songs to every cinema in the country, with a free issue of band parts.

Faced with a broadcasting monopoly it was no great change from the previous form of promotion to direct payment to broadcasting musicians, and publishers and songwriters unwilling to make such payments were simply left out. So great was the number of complaints about "plugging" that the BBC prohibited dance band leaders from speaking at the microphone. In 1933 a special official was appointed by the BBC to listen for plugging. He had the power to ban offenders from the air for periods of six months, but the problem remained and was a source of friction between PRS members and the BBC even after the Second World War [15]. These payments which offended the ethical standards of the thirties may be contrasted with the inducements of sexual gratification alleged by the prosecution to have been offered in order to promote a songwriter's new works in *R.v.Jones, Dee and Gilbert* [16].

Although as early as 1914 some of the biggest promoters of musical entertainments had accepted the claims of PRS and taken out its licence, including J. Lyons and the Savoy Hotel, a great number of music users remained firmly opposed to the collection of revenue in respect of the performing right, and declined to pay. So long as their efforts were not concerted, this posed no real problem to the Society, which dealt with them on an individual basis as one of the normal factors of business. Generally a solicitor's letter was enough to dispose of the matter at this level. But when these opponents banded together into organised groups, this posed a more serious threat to the Society.

Sometimes this facilitated negotiations, for then the Society could perhaps enter into a licensing arrangement with an association representing an entire trade or business group. Clearly once composers and publishers of music had formed an association to exploit their rights, it was a natural reaction that music users would unite in organisations for the protection of their interests. On the one hand, this increased

14 1928 Copyright Royalty (Mechanical Musical Instruments) Enquiry-Evidence of William Boosey.
15 Professor Asa Briggs, The History of Broadcasting in the United Kingdom,vol.2,p.86.
16 Tried at the Central Criminal Court, London, in December 1973.

licensees' bargaining powers, and on the other it lessened the trans-action costs of individual negotiations for the Society[17].

More intransigent users of music grouped themselves first into the British Music Union Ltd., which in 1919 had issued a catalogue of free music in an effort to strike down PRS in its infancy[18]. Linked with Parliamentary lobbying its members carried on a special campaign throughout the early twenties, until in 1927 a new and more compre-hensive organisation of music users was set up, known as the Inter-national Council of Music Users Ltd. Its membership was made up of a large number of hoteliers, restaurants, cafes, clubs, dance halls, corporations, cinemas and the Musicians Union[19]. It also included gramophone companies among its membership, for until the decision in *Gramophone Company Ltd. v. Stephen Carwardine Ltd.*[20], record manufacturers were not regarded as owning any rights in the nature of copyright, apart from a reproduction right.

After attempting to obtain bulk discounts on PRS tariffs, and failing, the International Council of Music Users in 1929 promoted through a private member of Parliament the Musical Copyright Bill, which was designed to undermine the effect of the *Copyright Act 1911*, in so far as it had revitalised the performing right in musical works.

There were two main proposals to be considered in the Bill. The first was to make it compulsory, in order to reserve the performing right, for the copyright owner to cause to be printed on the title page of all musical works published after the passing of the Bill a notice specifically reserving that right. This was an exact parallel with *S.1 Copyright (Musical Compositions) Act 1882*[21], and would have consti-tuted, had it reached the statute book, an infringement of British obligations under the Berne Convention. Although the original treaty had provided by *Art.2 Berne Convention 1882* that enjoyment of the rights conferred were to be "subject to the accomplishment of the conditions and formalities prescribed by the law of the country of origin of the work", it had been later decided by *Art.4 Berne Convention (Berlin Revision) 1908* that the enjoyment and exercise of copyright in the adhering states "shall not be subject to the performance of any formality". This is one of the reasons why the *Copyright (Musical*

---

17 Economists' Advisory Group,op.cit.,p.44.
18 See Chapter 6 ante.
19 Special Report from the Select Committee on the Musical Copyright Bill (1930) at question 461.
20 [1934] Ch.450.
21 See Chapter 5 ante.

Compositions) Acts 1882 and *1888* were repealed by the *Copyright Act 1911.* The provision was carried over into the Rome Revision, and the proposed amendment thus would have offended against Britain's international obligations in 1928. The corresponding paragraph is today *Art. 5 (2) Berne Convention (Paris Revision)* 1971.

The other provision of the Musical Copyright Bill was that a maximum fee of 2d. was to be payable as a consideration in perpetuity for the performing right in any musical work, to be payable on the purchase of a copy of the work. This measure, if enacted, would have completely undermined the concept of the performing right in musical works as it had been shaped by the *Copyright Act 1911,* for it was irrespective of the extent or nature of the work, or the size and character of the place of performance[22]. It would have applied to copies of a symphony and to the latest popular song with equal lack of discrimination, and by the same token to performances in a public bar or in the Albert Hall. A popular vocalist could have bought one copy of the latest successful song, and in theory could have given innumerable performances to audiences to the number of many thousands, and all for one royalty of 2d. The proposal would undoubtedly have destroyed PRS if it had been carried, and it is not surprising that it was described by its opponents as "that shameless and absurd measure "[23]. A. P. Herbert, as he then was, pointed out that the real intention of the Bill was to bring PRS to ruin[24]. Never short of articulate talent, the composers' and publishers' lobby was to coin for the instrument the derisive nickname of "The Tuppenny Bill"[25].

Nevertheless the Bill was given a second reading and referred to a Select Committee of the House of Commons. Fortunately for the Society, that Committee came to the following conclusion:

"Your Committee are agreed that a fixed fee cannot be applied to all the varying circumstances of public performance if the composer is to receive reasonable remuneration. Nor do they wish to place any obstacle in the way of composers forming an association for the purposes of protecting and enforcing their performing rights. Such an association is undoubtedly a convenience and almost a necessity, both to the composer, music publisher and the user of music who would undoubtedly be considerably embarrassed if he had to deal separately with each piece of music performed. In fact, it may be said to be the only practicable way in which the composer can collect his fees for

22 Unpublished records of PRS.
23 Daily Telegraph, 12th July 1930.
24 Punch, 4th December 1929.
25 Unpublished records of PRS.

performing rights in any adequate manner. If such an association is to function effectively, it must obtain as near a super-monopoly as is possible of the monopolies conferred upon composers by the Copyright Acts ''[26].

So parliament in effect set its seal of approval upon the existence of the Performing Right Society, but its reference to monopoly powers were ominous, and the Report went on to enlarge on this theme.

''Your Committee consider that such a super-monopoly can abuse its rights by refusing to grant licences upon reasonable terms so as to prejudice the trade or industry of persons carrying on business in this country and to be contrary to the public interest, and that it should be open to those persons to obtain relief in respect of such abuse by appeal to arbitration or to some other tribunal. This should apply only in those cases where the ownership or control of copyright has been transferred to an Association.''

The feeling by governments that some control of copyright collecting societies' monopoly position is required is by no means novel. The collecting society in Canada (now known as CAPAC), was set up in 1925, and as early as 1931 the Canadian Government introduced a system whereby any society carrying on in Canada the business of acquiring copyrights of dramatico-musical works or musical works, or performing rights therein, and which deals with or in the issue or grant of licences for the performance in Canada of such works is required to file an annual statement of its fees for the coming year. The Copyright Appeal Board set up under this system considers objections to the proposed fees, alters the statements as it thinks fit, and transmits those statements to the approprite minister. The minister publishes those statements in the Canada Gazette, and they are binding for the coming year ''[27].

It is surprising that both the current leading textbook on the subject [28], and the expert Gregory Committee which considered the proposals for the *Copyright Act 1956* [29], make no reference to the deliberations of the 1930 Select Committee on the Musical Copyright Bill. In particular it is unfortunate that the impression is left in both these classical source works on British copyright that the germ of the notion of an anti-monopoly tribunal somehow originated in Canada, shortly after the formation of a copyright collecting society in that country, when

26 Report of the Select Committee on the Musical Copyright Bill (1930).
27 McFarlane, Copyright Collecting Societies, Grove's Dictionary of Music and Musicians, 6th edn., (Macmillan).
28 Copinger and Skone James on Copyright, 11th edn., para.1061 et seq.
29 Report of the Copyright Committee, Cmnd.8662,1952,para.204 et seq.

117

clearly the idea had been considered in Parliament at Westminster at an earlier date[30].

In fact instructions were given to the Board of Trade (as it then was) as a result of the deliberations of the 1930 Select Committee to frame a policy for adoption at the next revision meeting of the Berne Convention "which would secure freedom for Her Majesty's Government to deal with any abuse of monopoly rights"[31].

Due to the Second World War, however, the next meeting for the revision of the Berne Union did not take place until 1948 in Brussels. But due to the fear of anti-monopoly measures being taken, the policy of PRS in its negotiations with music users was considerably moderated, which resulted in copyright royalties in the U.K. falling even further out of line with those in equivalent foreign countries[32]. This is apart from low fees already being asked by PRS on some tariffs because of its inhibitions during its early years of existence.

30 The setting up of the Performing Right Tribunal under the **Copyright Act 1956** is to be considered in a later chapter.
31 Economists Advisory Group,op.cit.,p.50.
32 Unpublished records of PRS.

9
Further extension of the Performing Right in case-law

By the end of the twenties PRS was beginning to establish itself in the public mind by its general activities, its Parliamentary campaigns, and also by its appearances in the High Court. Once this initial foundation had been laid, a policy of consolidation and interpretation of the rights involved was put in hand, and prominent among these cases was *Harms (Incorporated) and Chappell & Co. v. Martans Club Ltd* [1]. Following the decision in *PRS v. London Theatre of Varities* [2], the action was brought, not by the Society, but by the owners of copyright and the publishers of a work entitled "That Certain Feeling". The musical production of which the work formed a part had not yet been produced in the U.K., and no doubt in order to protect the novelty value of an extremely popular work, the publishers, presumably with the backing of PRS, moved at an early stage to obtain judicial clarification of the expression "performance in public".

The proprietors of the Embassy Club in Old Bond Street were the defendants. It was a fashionable establishment in the West End of London with a high subscription entitling its substantial membership to dine and dance on the premises. On the night in question 150 members had attended the club with some 50 guests, when for their entertainment a performance of the work in question was given by an orchestra. The plaintiffs brought an action for infringement of their copyright, claiming damages and an injunction. The defendants admitted the performance, but maintained that it was not in public. It had been held at first instance that the performance was within the meaning of the *Copyright Act 1911* [3].

On appeal the correct interpretation of the words "in public" in *S.1(2) Copyright Act 1911* was considered in detail, and although Lord Hanworth, then Master of the Rolls, considered *Wall v. Taylor* [4] and *Duck v. Bates* [5], he acknowledged that these dealt with the position

---

1 [1927] 1 Ch.326.
2 [1924] A.C.1.
3 [1926] Ch.870
4 11 QBD 102.
5 13 QBD 843.

under the *Dramatic Copyright Act 1833* and the *Literary Copyright Act 1842*, and the nature of a "place of dramatic entertainment". He was reassured by the fact that in both cases the court had felt that the decision had largely turned upon the facts of the particular case. He acknowledged that although the 1911 Act had granted the copyright owner a monopoly, the word was not to be used in any sinister sense.

The Master of the Rolls found that having regard to the nature of the club, and the entrance fee and subscription, the unauthorised performance of the work had caused injury to the plaintiffs. The type of persons resorting to the club were of a class likely to go to a place of public performance if an entrance fee had been required. He recited various tests which had been applied in previous cases on the subject, and said that one should try to see whether there had been any injury to the author. "Did what took place interfere with his proprietary rights? As to that, profit is a very important element." Accordingly he dismissed the appeal. The principle of profit had thus been opened up, and was due to be further extended in later cases.

Such an extension was made in *Performing Right Society v. Hawthorns Hotel (Bournemouth) Ltd*[6]. The defendant hotel owners had caused two musical works to be performed in the course of a programme by an orchestral trio in the lounge of their residential hotel. The audience consisted of a number of residential guests and an official of PRS, who, after giving notice of his wish to dine at the hotel, had in fact dined there accompanied by a friend, and had afterwards gone into the lounge with his friend and listened to the music.

It was argued on behalf of the defendants that the performance was not public because it was of a domestic or quasi-domestic nature, and the two persons who attended on behalf of PRS were not genuine members of the public, but were there to watch the interests of the plaintiffs. The report of the judgement of Bennett J. is unfortunately brief, and the reason given for his decision in the plaintiffs' favour was that any member of the public who had given notice to the defendants of his desire to dine at the hotel on the night of the infringement would in fact have been allowed to have dinner there, provided he appeared to be respectable. He would also it appears have been at liberty to go into the lounge and listen to the music performed by the trio. Accordingly, held the learned judge, the performance by the defendants constituted a performance in public, and one which infringed the plaintiffs' rights.

It would seem therefore that the decision was given solely on the attendance of the PRS inspector and his friend, who constituted the

---

6 [1933] Ch.855

members of the public, and that had they not been there, and had the audience consisted solely of residential guests of the hotel, the inference is that the performance would still have been held to be "public". It is the fact that this hotel was in theory open to any member of the public which enabled the judgement to be given for the Society.

A full examination of the authorities on the topic of performance in public was soon to be provided in *Jennings v.Stephens* [7]. This case involved neither musical works nor the Performing Right Society. The plaintiff was the author and the owner of copyright in a play called "The Rest Cure", and as there was no collecting society for dramatic works at that time, the author sued in her own name, although the League of British Dramatists did hold a watching brief. The play had been performed by a dramatic society in the parish of Duston, organised by the village branch of the Womens' Institute, part of a countrywide organisation of the National Federation of Womens' Institutes. There was an annual subscription of 2/-, with monthly meetings of an educational or social nature, and the female population of the village was 1085, of whom 109 were members of the Institute. 62 members of the Institute were present at the meeting where the performance took place, but apart from the 5 performers, no guests were present. The plaintiff sued for infringement of copyright, and at first instance it was held that the performance was quasi-domestic, the plaintiff accordingly failing.

The report is based on the appeal, and the leading judgement is that of the then Master of the Rolls, Lord Wright. He referred to the fact that the Federation of Womens' Institutes had circularised its member institutes advising them that the presence of visitors changed the performance from a private to a public one, whether or not a charge was made for admission. As no visitors were present at the performance in question, save for the actors who were themselves of a neighbouring institute, the defendant claimed that the performance was not in public. The Master of the Rolls clearly felt the decision in *Duck v. Bates* to be somewhat strained, the court there feeling sympathy for the alleged infringers who comprised largely the nursing staff of Guys Hospital. He distinguished that case from *Harms v. Martans Club* and *PRS v. Hawthorns Hotel (Bournemouth)*, on the basis that in the former case the audience was limited to a class more or less living under the same roof, while in the latter two the audience consisted of any members of the public who had accepted the invitation to attend, either by becoming members of the club or guests of the hotel.

---

7 [1936] Ch.469

The invitation to attend in either of these cases last mentioned was held to be to a portion of the public, although nevertheless that portion of the public was limited in class. The presence or absence of visitors was not the decisive factor, nor was it conclusive that admission was free or for payment, nor was the number of the audience held to be crucial. Further, it did not matter whether the performers were paid, or whether they gave their services gratuitously. There was no other qualification for membership of the Duston Womens' Institute apart from residence in the village, (and presumably also membership of the female sex); residence itself did not automatically render the audience domestic or quasi-domestic. Accordingly it was held that the performance in question was in public, and the appeal allowed.

This success, albeit engineered by the League of British Dramatists [8], was of extreme value to the Performing Right Society, and one which enabled it to adopt a far more confident line in negotiations with potential licensees. The importance was to be underlined a few years later by a significant judgement obtained in respect of special wartime arrangements in factories, which had resulted in the cases jointly reported as *Ernest Turner Electrical Instruments Ltd. v.PRS* and *PRS v. Gillette Industries Ltd* [9].

Shortly after the outbreak of the Second World War in September 1939, the BBC on its own initiative began a series of special programmes entitled "Music While You Work" for relay by loudspeakers to workers in factories, who at that time were working unusually long shifts, and were being urged to increase production. The idea was a great success, and the programme was to become one of the longest running in the history of British broadcasting. The extraordinary popularity of the experiment led to a demand for this background music not only in places of work, but also in places of entertainment. The beginning of this development was on a very muted scale, with a small number of outlets, and with the emphasis on unobtrusiveness [10].

As several of the great Departments of State had already concluded agreements with PRS in respect of their use of music for special wartime activities, the Society considered that it should charge at least nominal tariffs to commercial users of Music While You Work. This was resisted by certain employers, and two actions were brought on the issue. They were both heard at first instance by Bennett J., and the appeals came on together.

---

8 Now part of the Society of Authors
9 [1943]Ch.167
10 After the war, background music was rapidly to develop into an important part of the Society's business.

In the Turner case, the plaintiffs sought a declaration that the performance of music at their factory did not constitute an infringement of the Society's copyright. The Society contended that the plaintiffs had disclosed no cause of action, and sought an injunction to restrain the public performance of its musical works without its consent. The judge at first instance found in favour of the Society. In the Gillette case on the other hand the Society brought an action for an injunction on similar facts, and again Bennett J. found in favour of PRS. The factory owners in both cases appealed.

Lord Greene in finding for the Society relied on the case of *Jennings v. Stephens*, and in particular on the observation that the real criterion seems to be the true character of the audience. He found that in both cases before him the audience was formed of a substantial part of the working population of the district, which was clearly fond of music, and being supplied with something which it liked. That it assisted their work was irrelevant, for they were both working, and enjoying music as they would in their leisure hours. The legislature had given a monopoly to the copyright owner, and as a criterion of whether a performance was in public, the Master of the Rolls formed a test of whether the economic value of that monopoly was whittled down by the performance.

Applying that test, he had no doubt that the factory performance was in public. What took place within the factory was not purely the domestic concern of those within it. If similar performances were given in factories all over the British Isles without compensation to the copyright owner, it would destroy the value of his monopoly. The audience in each factory should therefore be regarded as a section of the public. In this judgement Goddard L. J. as he then was, concurred, observing that otherwise the benefits of the Copyright Act to the right owner would become largely illusory.

At the same period as *Jennings v. Stephens*, PRS was to gain a victory in another angle of attack which was also to increase its power considerably, a victory which also arose from the new medium of broadcasting by radio.

In *PRS v. Hammonds Bradford Brewery Ltd.*[11], although the legal argument and technical evidence was complex, the facts were comparatively simple. By a clause in its agreement with the infant British Broadcasting Corporation, PRS licensed not only the broadcasting of musical works in its repertoire, but also the "audition or reception of copyright musical works by means of broadcasting for domestic or

---

11 [1934]1 Ch.121

private use." In accordance with this agreement, three songs of which the Society was the copyright owner were performed by consent at a cinema, and that performance broadcast by the BBC. By means of a wireless set and a loudspeaker installed on the premises of a hotel, the works being broadcast were made available to visitors to the hotel. PRS brought an action for infringement alleging that the act of making audible in the hotel constituted a separate and infringing performance.

The question in the United States had been decided in favour of the copyright owners in *Buck v.Jewell-La Salle Realty Co* [12]. There it had been held that the making audible of the broadcast at the receiving end constituted a separate performance. In an action in Germany brought by the sister society of PRS, it had however been held impossible to dissociate the reception from the transmission. This was the case of *Musikschutzverband v.Reichskartell der Musikveranstalter Deutschlands e.V* [13].

The report of the English case contains both the hearing at first instance, and the judgement of the Court of Appeal. In the court below, Maugham J. found for PRS without great difficulty. The defendants had alleged that the use of a radio receiver and a loudspeaker as they had done was not a performance, or at any rate not a performance by themselves, but this argument had not attracted the puisne judge. On appeal, Lord Hanworth, then the Master of the Rolls, regarded the audience in the hotel as outside the defendants' domestic circle. The defendants urged once more that there had not been a performance by themselves, but that the only performance had taken place at the cinema where the works had actually been played. The listeners in the hotel, they contended, were merely an extension of the audience in the cinema, and had heard nothing more than the performance in the cinema. Lord Hanworth agreed that the defendants had by their installation of the special equipment made the performance at the cinema audible to a wider number of people than would otherwise have heard it, but as these people were outside the defendants' domestic circle, it amounted either to a performance, or the authorisation of a performance.

It was left to Romer L. J., whose judgements are among the most lucid in copyright cases of this period, to make the distinction which crushed the argument for the defence that what took place was nothing but an extension by technical aids to Huddersfield of the voice of the singer in London. No, retorted the Lord Justice, if the voice were extended from

12 [1931] 283 U.S. 191
13 Entscheidungen des Reichsgerichts in Zirilsachen, (1932), Band 136,no.74

London to Huddersfield, it would take some 15 minutes to travel the 200 miles, as vibrations in the air travel at 1000 feet per second. However, the sound waves in broadcasting travel at about 186,000 miles per second, perhaps enabling the sound to be heard in Huddersfield before it was heard by someone sitting at the back of the cinema. The two concepts were therefore quite different. Furthermore, PRS had never consented to the defendants making use in this manner of works in which it controlled the copyright. The appeal failed, fortunately for the Society, for defeat on this issue would have allowed wide secondary use of their works without payment.

PRS v. Camelo[14] carried the Brewery case a state further, and effectively sealed off further attempts to get round that decision. The defendant had the lease of premises upon which his wife operated a restaurant in one room of the ground floor. The defendant and his family used an adjoining room solely as a living-room, which formed no part of their business enterprise. However, in that room the defendant had placed a wireless set which was played so loudly that it was audible to his customers in the restaurant room adjoining, and there was evidence that the customers had derived entertainment from it. The defendant contended that it was quite fortuitous if the performance had been heard in the restaurant, but this was treated as a question of fact, and decided in favour of the plaintiff.

Clauson J. considered that once the wireless receiver reproduced the music in a particular area, the ensuing performance took place wherever that music was audible to a person hearing it as a musical piece. Although the performance in this case took place in a private living-room, it extended beyond that area throughout the restaurant, which was of course public. He therefore found that the plaintiff's rights had been infringed, the performance amounting to a performance in public within the meaning of the Act.

Copinger and Skone-James[15] notes the case as deciding that a performance on private premises is a performance in public where it was so performed with the object of it being heard in public. It is with respect suggested that this is not an accurate summary of the result of the decision, and that the element of intention is not a requisite to a performance in public within the meaning of the Act. Clauson J. did not place this limitation upon his judgement. Indeed he records that "all sorts of suggestions were put to me as to what might happen if a person passing

---

14 [1936] 3 All. E.R. 557
15 Copyright, 11th edn., para.515 (note)

along a road was listening to a performance on a wireless set he might hear'', so that he was aware of the ultimate lengths to which his decision might be taken. He based it on the area within which the performance could be heard, not upon the intention of the person giving the performance. Strictly applied, *S.2(5)(c)Copyright Act 1956* applies to the owner of a loudly played transistor on Brighton beach, or even in his own garden. Whether he intends it or not, he is giving a public performance for which PRS could strictly demand a royalty. That they choose not to exercise their rights in certain cases is a matter for their discretion - they may consider that the difficulties of enforcement would be impracticable in certain cases, in others the administrators feel that delicacy demands that the right should not be put into effect, as is the case in performances during services of divine worship.

For some thirty years after the Turner/Gillette cases, the officials of the Society went about their business secure in the feeling that whatever else might be challenged successfully, the basis and extent of the performing right on which their whole operation was founded would not be upset by the courts. In 1973 they were to receive a rude shock when the judgement of the Outer House of the Court of Session was handed down in *PRS v. Rangers Supporters Club, Greenock*.[16]

Lord Stott gave judgement on 2nd May, referring to three compositions controlled by the pursuers (plaintiffs) having been performed on the premises of the defenders (defendants), without a licence having been obtained from the Society. Of the audience of some 150, 25 were guests of members. The club had been formed for social purposes among the members, and to make travel arrangements to football matches in which Glasgow Rangers Football Club was playing, membership being confined to supporters. He observed that the term ''in public'' had not been defined in the *Copyright Act 1956*, and referred to the construction which had been placed upon it in earlier cases in England. Though none were binding upon him, he recorded that he would treat them as of persuasive authority, and accordingly accepted that the performances of a work in a proprietory club such as in *Harms v. Martans*, in a lounge as in *PRS v. Hawthorns Hotel*, at a meeting of the Womens' Institute as in *Jennings v. Stephens* and on the factory floor as in *Turner v. PRS* were all performances in public.

What it all came to, concluded Lord Stott, was that the court having determined as a matter of law the meaning of ''in public'', it must make up its mind on the facts of each case whether the performance in

---

16 1973 SLT 198 at first instance

question fell within that meaning. None of the English cases cited was in his view directly on the point which he had to decide, and he drew a distinction between private clubs simpliciter, and private clubs established for profit. He considered that while it might be reasonable to protect an author against the performance of his work in a club which purveys entertainment for the proprietor's profit or in a hotel lounge or on the factory floor or to a Womens' Institute, membership of which, he said, is open to every woman in the village, he did not find that it followed to extend protection to a performance by a members' club for their own entertainment. In his view a club was by definition an association of persons in private. The element of privacy was absent when the club was nothing more than a collection of members of the public prepared to pay the proprietors an annual subscription in return for having music provided for their entertainment, but that was not the position of the Rangers Supporters Club.

His Lordship's view was that its membership was selective, there was no invitation to the public or entertainment provided to the public for the financial benefit of a proprietor, and no public advertisement. The defendants, he found, were providing entertainment for themselves on their own premises and that in his opinion had more of the flavour of a private than a public performance. Therefore on the facts of this case, he found that there was no public performance.

It is hard to differentiate between the criteria applied by Lord Stott and the facts of *Jennings v.Stephens*, where there was no invitation to the public, no entertainment for the financial benefit of a proprietor, and no public advertisement. Just as much as the Rangers Supporters Club, the Womens' Institute had been providing entertainment for themselves. If that was now to be held to be a private performance it would be a grievous blow to the Society, which estimated that the loss of income from members' clubs in the North of England alone would amount to £3000. Clearly the matter had to be taken to appeal without delay.

The judgement of the Scottish appeal court was given on 11th December 1973 [17]. Lord Milligan took issue with the judgement of Lord Stott; in particular he disagreed with the observation in the court below that what the defendants were doing was providing entertainment on their own premises for themselves and their guests, and the conclusion that this appeared to have more the flavour of a private performance than one in public. As had Lord Stott, Lord Milligan considered that

17 [1975] R.P.C.626.

Parliament had not defined the phrase "in public", so that the courts might decide each case according to its special circumstances. Copyright both protected the composer from unauthorised reproduction or plagiarism, and also prevented third parties from using the work to the author's financial disadvantage. This, observed Lord Milligan, was generally of more financial benefit to the author, for he was generally paid for this right.

He found that the key to the matter lay in the consideration of the earlier cases of whether a particular performance was quasi-domestic; the answer was found in the relationship between the audience and the copyright owner. Where a person organised a private party in his own home, or what might reasonably be regarded as an extension of his home, that is not to the financial disadvantage of the author, since the selected audience is not enjoying his musical work under conditions in which they would normally pay for the privilege in one form or another. That would be an example of a private performance. A members' club along the lines of the Supporters' Club, albeit it that it made no profits, could not be regarded as an extension of the hospitality which each member might provide for himself as an individual or extend to his guests in his own private home. The circumstances there were more similar to a public place like an hotel, restaurant or dance-hall where the law of copyright might apply. Lord Milligan therefore held that the performance in question had been in public, adding that to hold otherwise would be to destroy the protection which the 1965 Act set out to confer on the copyright owner.

Thus the Society's position had been restored, to its very considerable relief, but it had been an unpleasant experience for those in control. The judgement of Lord Milligan is perhaps clearer than any of the English cases from the thirties, in particular his test of whether the selected audience is enjoying the author's work under conditions in which it would normally pay for that privilege in some form. It seems unlikely that a lower court in the U.K. can now reasonably find against the Society in an infringement case in which both title and performance are admitted. PRS has recently had other aspects of litigation to concern itself about, but these are in the field of anti-monopoly law, and will be considered in a later chapter [18].

Some areas will remain where PRS has for some time declined to exercise the rights vested in it in a particular area, and then a change of mind has occurred because of changed circumstances. An example recently took place in the case of *PRS v. Harlequin Record Shops Ltd.*

18 See Chapter 12 post.

[*1979*] 2 All E.R. 828[19]. Prior to 1976 the Society did not require owners of record shops to obtain licences to play records of the Society's works in their shops. Previously such records had generally been played in individual booths to customers, but the shopkeepers had introduced the practice of virtually perpetual playing of records over amplified speakers which all the shoppers could hear, and frequently many passers by.

The defendant company contended that such playing did not constitute a performance in public as potential purchasers of the records were not part of the composers' public, and that the exclusive right of public performance granted by the composer to the Society was subject to an implied reservation to the composer of the right to license record shops to play records of their works to promote sales of the records. This contention did not attract Browne-Wilkinson J., who granted PRS an injunction against the playing of such records without payment of a royalty to the Society.

---

19 [1979] 2 All E.R.828.

10
Phonographic Performance Limited and the performing right in records

From 1914 onwards a student of the performing right in Britain would be forgiven for thinking that the whole story thereafter is simply a history of the Performing Right Society. This is in fact very nearly the case. PRS quickly set up a country-wide network of operation, it gained the benefit of affiliation with established societies in other countries and thus could control their works in Britain, and it also benefited from the strong lobby of famous composers and powerful publishers who at last decided to throw their weight behind a copyright collecting organisation in a way which their counterparts in France had been doing for well over a century.

In the absence of a similar operation in the field of dramatic literature, PRS was virtually on its own, until in the 1930's there took place a development in the U.K. which was at that time unique, in the shape of an allegation that a performing right existed in favour of the manufacturers of a gramophone record in respect of the playing of that record in public. Although the right has taken root in certain parts of the world, it cannot be said to be flourishing, and in many areas it has been totally rejected, there is reason to think now that it is past its peak, and may be declining in terms of its acceptance by governments.

S.19(1) Copyright Act 1911 had provided "Copyright shall subsist in records, perforated rolls and other contrivances by means of which sounds may be mechanically reproduced, in like manner as if such contrivances were musical works, but the term of the copyright shall be fifty years from the making of the original plate." When the introduction of this section had been considered by the 1909 Copyright Committee, representatives of the gramophone manufacturing industry had considered, so they said to the Committee, that the purchaser of a gramophone record acquired with his purchase any right of public performance in that record[1]. This would mean that the purchaser could

---

1 Copyright Committee 1909, Report, paras. 1130-1132.

play his record either in public or in private, without incurring any further obligations.

For over twenty years this was the accepted position, and no one questioned it, least of all the record makers. But by the early thirties the general recession had begun to hit record sales. "Economic factors were responsible for the cutting of salaries; the talking films were putting many musicians out of work, and the Roaring Twenties were giving way to the Depressed Thirties "[2]. The record companies began to cast around anxiously for an additional form of income to bolster their sagging profits; the success of the Performing Right Society had not gone unnoticed, nor had the considerable use of records in broadcasting passed their attention. The largest firm of record manufacturers in Britain, at that time also the largest company in the world, collected evidence of the performance in public in a restaurant in the West of England of a record made by them. They brought an action against the proprietors of the restaurant for the infringement of their performing right in the record. The action is reported as *Gramophone Company v. Carwardine*[3].

It was argued that *S.19 Copyright Act 1911* merely protected the manufacturers[4]. The judge, Maugham J., complained of the defective nature of the section which he was construing, but in relation to the phrase "in like manner as if such contrivances were musical works", he was adamant that it did not exist merely to prevent the reproduction of the record in a physical form, or the right to sell the record. He held firmly that the owner of the right created under the section is the owner of the sole right to use that record for a performance in public. The judgement was never appealed or reversed, and it was taken to be a correct statement of the position from 1911, until 1956, when the judgement was clothed in statutory form by *S.12 Copyright Act 1956*.

Shortly after this decision in 1934, Phonographic Performance Limited, abbreviated to PPL, was set up by the record companies to administer the new right as a company limited by guarantee and without share capital, controlling the public use of their records and issuing licences in connection therewith. All revenue from licence royalties is distributed not only among the record companies, but ex gratia payments are also made to recording artistes, musicians and copyright

---

2 Rex Harris, "Jazz", (Pelican 1952),p.108.
3 [1934] 1 Ch.450.
4 The activity now known as "piracy".

owners. The basis of distribution arrived at when PPL was set up was 20% of the nett distributable revenue for the benefit of the recording artistes, 12% for the Musicians Union and a further 10% for the music publishers[5].

Thus since 1934 it has been necessary for people giving public performances by means of gramophone records to obtain a licence not only from the owner of the copyright in the music, generally through PRS, but also another licence from the record manufacturer through PPL. Similar organisations exercising the record manufacturer's right under the domestic laws of those countries exist in Australia, Germany, India, New Zealand and Scandinavia; in the case of the latter there is a single society in Copenhagen collecting for Denmark and Sweden [6].

When the Copyright Commission of 1951 examined the potential danger of the collecting societies' monopoly position, it devoted close attention to the operations of PPL, and expressed severe criticism of some of the practices adopted by it. The members put their fingers directly on to the sore point, the volte-face of the record companies in relation to the right in records which since 1934 has been of considerable embarrassment to the gramophone companies.

Reference was made to the evidence given to the Copyright Committee 1909[7], the conclusions of which had led to the *Copyright Act 1911*. The 1951 Committee stated "It seems incontrovertible to us that already in the year 1909 public performances of gramophone records, despite their technical deficiencies, were taking place, and that the case put by the gramophone companies was that the composers' new rights given under the Convention should be merged with the new rights sought by the companies, so that any customer who bought a record should be allowed to play it as and when he chose, in public or in private, without incurring any further obligation [8]."

The question which the 1951 Committee set itself to answer was "whether the right of public performance as hitherto enjoyed and as interpreted in the Courts is unreasonably wide or has been exercised in a manner prejudicial to the public interest "[9]. So far as PPL was concerned, the Commission was unimpressed with the change of heart which had led to the formation of a new collecting society. Although the

---

5 Economists Advisory Group, op.cit.,p.65
6 McFarlane, Copyright Collecting Societies, Grove's Dictionary of Music and Musicians, 6th edn., (Macmillan).
7 Para, 1130 onwards.
8 Cmnd.8662,para.142.
9 Cmnd.8662,para.122 & 123.

authority was not cited to the 1951 Committee members, the general view prior to 1934 is to be found stated in earlier editions of the leading British copyright textbook of recent decades; "the intention probably was to prevent one record from being copied directly or indirectly from another record "[10]. The view is put more clearly in the latest edition; "it was originally supposed that this right was to protect manufacturers against copying of their recordings by rival manufacturers"[11].

The Committee members were not surprised by the admission of one witness that he found the necessity of trying to control the record manufacturers' right embarrassing[12]. The Committee seemed to place PRS and PPL in different categories because, while the former never refused licences to prospective licensees, PPL frequently did. The Committee members found repugnant the attempt by the manufacturer to control the uses to which his product was put after it had been bought and paid for by his customer, and they observed that if this principle were to be observed generally in trade, it would produce astonishing results. They appeared reluctant to place a mere product of manufacture such as a gramophone record on the same level as "an original literary, dramatic, musical or artistic work", adopting apparently the attitude of Continental jurists that the true authors' right is sacred, and quite apart from mere creatures of commerce which, if at all worthy of protection, must be saved by special statutes altogether on a lower plane than classical copyright [13]. Starkly put, "In France there exists in law no neighbouring right whereby, not only the performing artiste, but gramophone record manufacturers and broadcasting organisations are protected."

The Committee members were particularly impressed by the bitter attack made on PPL by the National Council of Social Service which, on behalf of a very large number of voluntary organisations of all types, complained of the arbitrary manner in which licences were withheld or withdrawn. Scout groups, Womens' Institutes, Y.M.C.A. and Y.W.C.A. joined in complaining about the conduct of the PPL management, which had rarely sought to justify its actions. Accordingly, "the conclusion to which we have been irresistibly driven as a result of our consideration of this evidence is that the rights have been enforced in an arbitrary and autocratic manner, with the minimum of consideration, and that whatever other changes may be required in connection

---

10 Copinger and Skone James, The Law of Copyright, (8th edn.) para 240
11 Copinger & Skone James,op.cit., (11th edn.) para.775
12 Cmnd.8662, para.143
13 Dr. Marie-Claude Dock, Étude sur le Droit d'Auteur,p.167

with the copyright provisions contained in *S.19 Copyright Act 1911*, some way must be found of limiting by statute the opportunities of exploitation flowing from the present interpretation of the term "public performance" in this connection "[14].

The Committee in its report arrived at certain conclusions on copyright collecting societies in general which will be examined in depth later in this study. So far as PPL was concerned, it might have been expected, in view of the severity of the complaints made against it in evidence and found to be sustained by the Committee members, that there would have been a clear recommendation that the scope of its right should be cut back, or repealed altogether. In fact this turned out not to be the case, and the Committee recommended that the performing right in gramophone records established by the Carwardine case should not be taken away from the manufacturers [15] . But the sharp criticism of PPL shows that this conclusion was only reached after considerable heart-searching by the Committee members. The consideration which apparently swayed the balance was that total lack of control might make the profession of musician still less attractive, and therefore in the long run the public would lose.

But a clear distinction was drawn between "true copyright", and the so-called "neighbouring right" of the record manufacturers. "To begin with we wish to make it clear that we regard the rights we recommend for broadcast programmes or gramophones as subsidiary to the primary right of the composer or author of the copyright work reproduced by these technical means, and that the performing rights in programmes or records should be without prejudice to that primary right. (The composer's right to authorise the recording or broadcasting of his work is, of course, unaffected.) In so far as it may be necessary to do so, we recommend that this principle should be recognised in any future legislation. We think that consideration should be given to the question whether rights of this kind should not be described by some term distinguishing them from copyright in its primary sense "[16].

In fact this distinction was not really made in the resulting legislation. If the Parliamentary draftsman made a conscious division between conventional copyright and the new neighbouring rights, it was so subtle as to be almost indistinguishable. It has been said by staunch supporters of the classical performing right that the word "works" is only used in relation to the four kinds of works protected under Part I of the 1956 Act,

---

14 Cmnd.8662,para.150
15 Cmnd.8662,para.184
16 Cmnd.8662,para.181

that is literary, dramatic, musical or artistic works, and that by not using the term in Part II, which talks merely of "copyright in sound recordings, cinematograph films, broadcasts, etc.", the distinction proposed by the Copyright Committee has been satisfied. But with respect this argument seems more ingenious than convincing.

Flushed with their success in the Carwardine case, the gramophone manufacturers set up an international pressure group called the International Federation of the Phonographic Industry (IFPI). Its brief was to lobby governments around the world for the introduction in their domestic laws of rights similar to those awarded to the manufacturers in the Carwardine case, and now encapsulated in *S.12 Copyright Act 1956*. The line that they took with the then British Dominions and Colonies was that the Carwardine case had decided that the record makers were entitled to a royalty in respect of the public performance of the record by virtue of *S.19(1)Copyright Act 1911*; so far as the colonies were concerned, *S.25(1)* Copyright Act 1911 expressly extended the provisions of that Act to the colonies and therefore they were caught by the Cawardine decision; in the case of the Dominions it was contended that as they had mainly passed laws which bordered closely on the 1911 Act of the U.K., they should in general apply U.K. decisions interpreting its application. By and large they did.

Virtually every Crown colony entered into some form of contract in respect of the performance by its broadcasting stations of records which often formed a very large part of the total broadcasting time. In those days no one locally was ever prepared to dispute a decision clothed with the authority of the British courts, and many such contracts were agreed on behalf of the colonies which were very favourable indeed to the record manufacturers.

The Dominions also paid up before the Second World War, and for a long time afterwards. When they passed new copyright acts following the 1956 Act in Britain, they tended to include the performing right in records. So large sums of money started to flow through the coffers of IFPI, which to this extent could be regarded as a collecting society, although its administrators never considered it as such. But there was little analysis of performance, and agreements were usually fixed for lump sum payments on an ad-hoc basis.

The chief function of IFPI was the lobbying of governments outside the Commonwealth to introduce performing rights in records. As long ago as the Berlin conference in 1908 for the revision of the Berne Convention, the U.K. delegation had raised the question of whether international protection might not be given to "gramophone discs, pianola rolls, and so on '' . It was then pointed out that the matter was on the borderline between industrial property and copyright, and might be held to belong more properly to the former category. The British interest lay in having at that time very much the largest share of the world market in records, and what it was then seeking was international protection against unauthorised copying of records. The British delegation raised the matter again at the 1928 Revision Conference in Rome with equal lack of success. Then in 1935 the Italian Government called an international conference to draw up a separate convention to protect gramophone records. Due to the Italian invasion of Abyssinia at the time, the conference was boycotted by most interested countries, and it did not take place.

After the Second World War, pressure began to mount from the record producers for the right in international law, and broadcasters and performers also called for international protection in their fields. It was decided to examine the possibilities of a joint convention, and a period of intense activity set in for IFPI.

Britain still enjoyed in the 1950's a dominant position in the field of record manufacture, and she still probably had the greatest interest in international recognition of a kind of performing right in favour of the product. But during this decade the efforts of the Federation reached their zenith, and a number of states began to introduce the performing right in records into their legislation. Canada had already introduced the right in its Act of 1952, but it was never exercised until 1968, subsequently to be realised as a great mistake by the gramophone interests. Czechoslovakia embodied the principle in its law of 1953, and Brazil a similar right in 1961. Headway was also made in Scandinavia where Denmark introduced the right in 1961, just following Sweden which had done the same in 1960. In certain other countries, such as Austria, Belgium, France and Holland, while the right had no legal recognition, voluntary payments in respect of record use were made to IFPI by the broadcasting organisations. This contrasted strangely with the fierce opposition of government in, for example, France [18],[19,20].

---

17 Professor Ulmer, The Rome Convention.
18 This account is largely based on McFarlane, ''The Rome Convention'' a thesis presented to the University of Sheffield for the degree of **LLM**. Other works on the topic which may be consulted are:-
19 Professor Ulmer, ''The Rome Convention: Work of the Conference, Previous History and Outcome.'' Also:-
20 Namurois, ''The International Convention for the Protection of Performers, Producers of Phonograms and Broadcasting Organisations'', (1962 European Broadcasting Review.)

The Convention was signed in Rome on 26th October 1961, providing, amongst other things, for a performing right in records. Very few states have adhered to it, and even fewer are applying the principle of international accounting in respect of the right. Indeed, this aspect of the Convention has only ever operated as between the U.K., West Germany, Denmark and Sweden.

The gramophone interests never managed to persuade the United States to introduce a performing right in records into their domestic copyright law. Had they done so, the recent history of neighbouring rights might have been much more successful. In recent years the field of copyright in America has been taken up with proposals for reform, for there had been no substantial change in the principal statute of the subject since 1909[21]. Many conflicting interests had been locked in dispute over the various issues for years, with the result that general reform had scarcely advanced since proposals for a wide overhaul were first made, in the late fifties.

A series of studies of the American copyright system was made then, and an overall revision bill based on these studies was introduced in 1964 which, with various subsequent revisions, was long pending in Congress. There were extensive, if not interminable, hearings on the subject in the Senate Judiciary Subcommittee on Patents, Trademarks and Copyrights, of which the result was "Further hearings, further modifications, and an increase in the heat generated by the conflicting interests. As the various forces became better organised and gave closer attention to the issues involved, they seemed to pull further apart and harden their positions"[22]. However, none of the proposed revisions in the Bill went further than protecting sound recordings against unauthorised reproduction; the performing right in records has never achieved the status of a proposal worthy of serious consideration in the United States, and this has been confirmed by its express exclusion in Section 114 of the new U.S. Statute passed in 1976.

In America therefore there was nothing for the gramophone interests to lose in relation to neighbouring rights. But that was not the case in Canada. The Canadian *Copyright Act 1921* contained the same provision as that on which the manufacturers had relied in the Carwardine case. For many years they did not attempt to exercise it. Apparently, until IFPI became interested in the situation, the local subsidiaries of the main gramophone companies had taken the view that they were

---

21 United States Code, Title 17.
22 Professor John C. Stedman, "Copyright Developments in the U.S."; Law in the United States of America in Social and Technological Revolution (1974) p.306

providing broadcasting stations with free copies of records, and were competing with each other to induce the stations to transmit their records; if successful in this aim, the companies considered that they would derive valuable publicity.

During attempts to save neighbouring rights in Australia and Malaysia, and to introduce them in America, IFPI was taunted with the fact that it had never dared to exercise the rights it already enjoyed in the law of Canada. In a desperate attempt to save the situation in these vital areas, it threw all its efforts into the Canadian campaign. In 1968 a company called Sound Recording Licences Limited (SRL) was set up by IFPI and issued a tariff of fees for performances of records which it submitted to the Copyright Appeal Board for approval. At the same time the Canadian government introduced a Senate Bill for the purpose of abolishing the performing right in records. Both sides then paused to await the report of the Economic Council of Canada on the subject, which had been charged with consideration of the issue in 1966. The report appeared in 1971, and was disastrous for IFPI.

"We continue to accept the concept of a performing right in the basic material because this is the only way in which a writer of such materials can get payment related to the use of his work in the market. The record maker, on the other hand, in spite of many creative "inputs" by his staff, is really in the business of selling a physical item such as a disc or tape, and it is this activity which should reimburse him. To say that he merits an extra fee each time his physical unit is publicly used is rather like saying that a book publisher should be paid an extra amount each time the book is read . . . Because the present Canadian law does allow a potential for such a right in sound recordings, we suggest it be removed "[23].

It was accurate to categorise the record manufacturers' product as a physical thing, rather than a work of creation, but the analogy with a book is unhappy. They failed to complete the equation by referring to a public reading of a book, as they had referred to a public performance of a record. Clearly there would be no royalty for a private reading of a book, just as the record manufacturers did not claim a royalty for a private playing of their records. On the other hand, if a writer had assigned copyright including a performing right in a play or novel to a publisher, it is the publisher who is entitled to the performing right if the work is read aloud in public.

The blow to IFPI from the 1971 Report re-opened an old wound given by the 1957 Copyright Commission, which had stated "The act

---

23 Economic Council of Canada, Report on Intellectual and Industrial Property 1971.

restricted by the copyright in a sound recording should be the making of a record embodying the recording. At the present time it would appear that an unauthorised public performance of a recording embodied in a record is an infringement of the copyright embodied in the record . . . We recommend the abolition of a record manufacturer's performing right . . . These rights are not exercised at the present time and if they were exercised it would probably be through some association or society. This is the way in which the public performing right in records is exercised in the United Kingdom. The existence and exercise of the right there have caused difficulties which are set out in the report of the Gregory Committee and we would not like to see a development of this kind in Canada"[24].

Although some hope was raised for IFPI when the Copyright Appeal Board approved their proposed tariffs for SRL with modifications in June 1971, the evidence which had been led on behalf of the record manufacturers sealed the fate of the right in the Canadian Parliament soon afterwards. "The initial impression one could have had of SRL as the champion of a domestic recording industry fostering Canadian talent was not supported by the evidence adduced in the course of the proceedings before the Copyright Appeal Board; the picture which emerged was more that of an industry controlled from abroad carrying out most of its substantial sales operations with records pressed in Canada from masters produced abroad, and having shown in the past very little concern for the development of Canadian talent or of a domestic record industry"[25].

The final submissions of SRL and its sponsors had an air of hopelessness. No one, they argued, should be allowed to use someone else's property for profit without being required to pay, falling back on the line that although the physical entity of the record had been sold, there was a creative element in the sounds in some way similar to arrangements and translations in which they retained the right of performance. Further, they contended, the Senate Bill amounted to an unjustified interference with a private conflict between the commercial interests of the broadcasters on the one side, and of the record manufacturers on the other [26]. Not surprisingly, these submissions did not prevail, and the Bill became law with effect from 1st January 1971.

---

24 Report of the Isley Commission on Copyright 1957,pp.77,78
25 Alleyn, "The Canadian Phonographic Industry deprived of its Performing Right in Canada.", 6 CPR 258
26 Alleyn, op.cit.,p.267.

In those few countries where the right now remains, its continuance is at best problematic, and must be at general risk whenever a particular domestic copyright statute comes up for revision. Even in the U.K. where it originated it may not last indefinitely, for reaction to it in the rest of the world is markedly stronger now than it was in 1951 at the time of the Gregory Committee. The British gramophone industry moreover is now no longer in the same dominating position as it was at that time, both at home and abroad, and foreign manufacturers have made huge inroads into markets which were formerly considered British preserves, to the extent that the balance of payments in respect of the performing right in records under the Rome Convention 1961 as between Britain and West Germany is no longer so heavily in favour of Britain.

Against this state of developments, and having regard to the unfavourable comments about the practices of PPL made by the Copyright Committee 1951 in Britain, it is not inconceivable that the right may eventually be repealed in this country. The position will then revert to that acquiesced in by the representatives of the gramophone industry themselves in 1909, when giving evidence to the Copyright Committee of that year.

"(Chairman-Lord Gorrell). Let us understand the position, that the purchaser of a disc should not merely acquire the right to use it in his own private surroundings like the singing of a song, but to use it in public? Yes.

And therefore to perform the songs publicly? Yes. We think it is perfectly reasonable to grant that concession. It is not a matter that would affect us directly as manufacturers, but it would affect a considerable number of our clients and customers.

Then, buying any rights from the author originally would include that right of public performance on the part of any purchaser of the disc from the manufacturers? Not that we should have to buy it separately, but that it should be understood to be a part of the sale of the phonographic print "[27].

---

27 Copyright Committee 1909, Minutes of Evidence,paras.1130-1132

9   The PRS' former headquarters [1934 - 1959] at 33 Margaret Street,
London.

11

Subsequent History of the Performing Right Society

By contrast with the experience of PPL, the Society gradually increased its acceptance by both music users and the general public. By moderate claims which it was careful not to operate in an arbitrary manner, mere toleration changed with the passing of the years to a position of some prestige. By 1971 PRS had been awarded the Queen's Award to Industry, and the Prince of Wales had accepted an invitation to be the guest of honour at the annual Members' lunch.

This increasing acceptance grew in relation to the Society's success in the Courts, but there were setbacks along the way, to such an extent that at times the successful exploitation of the performing right by an organised society in this country seemed to be in peril.

If the PRS directors had not been aware at the setting up of their company in 1914 that it was desirable for the Society to be the legal owner of the performing right in musical works which they purported to control, the adverse judgement in *PRS v. London Theatre of Varieties* [1] undoubtedly made them so [2]. At several of the Society's early general meetings alterations were made to its articles of association which went some way towards strengthening the position of PRS, but which nevertheless did not make it the effective legal owner of the performing right. There was considerable resistance to the proposal among publishers, and indeed in the early days some made it an express condition of joining the Society that they retained the full legal ownership of the performing right, and granted to PRS a mere licence.

This position was altered in 1926 by an Extraordinary General Meeting so that members assigned the Performing Right to the Society, unless on joining they specifically reserved it to themselves. However, not until 1934 was PRS strong enough to insist that all members should make a full assignment of their performing rights to it, and that no reservation should thereafter be permitted to a member [3].

---

1 [1924]A.C.I.
2 See Chapter 7 ante.
3 Unpublished Records of PRS.

The publishers had no cause to regret this decision, for from that point the Society never looked back. It had fought the main cases to establish the extent of the performing right within a short space of time, and thereafter litigation, with one or two major exceptions, became dominated by infringement actions against a permanent minority of persistent infringers, generally of an insubstantial nature. Income and distributions to members increased on the one hand, and on the other administrative costs were reduced.

This is in marked contrast to the experiences of PPL, and also of the Mechanical Copyright Protection Society (MCPS), which administers the "Mechanical right" of production on record arising under S.2(5)(a) *Copyright Act 1956* in favour of composers and publishers of music. In both cases the copyright owners retain the relevant parts of the copyright, and appoint the collecting society merely as their agent. There is no doubt that both these organisations have been far less effective in enforcing and collecting royalties than PRS, and that this is largely due to their weaker negotiating positions[4].

From the original PRS membership of 39 in 1914, numbers had grown to 291 by 1926 when the popular music publishers resumed their participation[5], and by 1930 the figure had grown to 1015[6]. While this gave the Society the greater part of the repertoire of British music at that time, nevertheless a sizeable and determined minority of influential publishers persisted in remaining outside. These were publishers whose catologues were substantially composed of educational and sacred music, and whose markets had been less affected by the gramophone record and by broadcasting. Their income from sheet music still held very firm, and led by Novellos, they had fiercely opposed the Society's proposed licensing arrangements with religious bodies for the use of music in secular entertainments. The following announcement was made. "As the chief object of the publication of music is to ensure performance, it does not seem reasonable to tax the performer for doing the very thing the publisher wants him to do. Messrs. Novello therefore do not belong to the Performing Right Society[7]"

Use of the words "tax" is an emotional one frequently met with in contentions of opponents of the right. It is an incorrect use, for the word imports an imposition of central government, enforced by law to raise

4 McFarlane, Copyright Collecting Societies, Grove's Dictionary of Music and Musicians,(6th edn.) (Macmillan).
5 See Chapter 6 ante.
6 Economists Advisory Group,op.cit.,pp.40/41
7 Musical Times, 1st December 1929, p.1073

revenue for the Exchequer. But at that time the word suited Novellos purpose, for they had continued to rely on the old technique of employing the performing right as a means of defence from borrowed, second-hand or hired copies of sheet music. Curiously, though, Novellos did not extend the free use principle to the broadcasting of their works, itself a clear indication that broadcasting was affecting this market[8].

But losses on sheet music eventually began to bite for this category of publisher, for on those who had remained outside PRS there were in addition the extremely high costs of individual negotiation with the BBC and other music users. Eventually in 1936 Novellos brought themselves to join PRS, and the firm made the following announcement. "Music of all kinds, including the best, is now used in a great number of places, and for a variety of purposes that would have been considered unlikely a decade ago. As some of these developments (e.g. that of music for film purposes) are clearly destined to become widespread, it is manifestly impossible for the interests of publishers and composers to be protected under the individual system that was formerly adequate. Moreover, collection of fees in foreign countries is more adequately done by the PRS in concert with similar foreign bodies. Composers who have in print any substantial number of works will be well advised to follow the example of the publishers and join the Society "[9].

Many others followed the lead set by Novellos, so that the membership of the Society went from 1,374 in 1935 to 1,861 in 1939, and its administrators felt able to claim that "recognition of the central principle of the collection of performing right fees through a central organisation became unanimous"[10].

On the licensing side, there were in 1919 some 4,400 licensees: by 1939 the figure had grown to 41,000, and the whole economic position of the British composer had changed in the interim. Before the establishment of PRS he had generally sold his rights for what was usually a fixed sum, but now the successful composer of popular works could earn a fortune in a matter of months from performing right royalties. Perhaps more important, the composer of serious music could now in a number of cases expect to live by his work[11]. As the profitable side of successful serious music tends to be longer than that of popular works, this represented a significant advance for composers in the former category.

Coupled with its rapid expansion inside the U.K., PRS had begun to interest itself increasingly in international affairs. In 1926 the Societé

8 Economists' Advisory Group,op.cit.,p.42
9 Musical Times, January 1936
10 C. F. James, "The Story of the PRS", (1951), p.79.
11 The P. R. Gazette, 1924

des Auteurs Dramatiques, the oldest collecting society in the world[12], had convened a meeting in Paris of representatives of dramatic authors' societies from some eighteen countries, which led to the formation of an International Confederation of Societies of Dramatic Authors. The U.K. was not represented; she had no such society then, the Dramatic Authors Society having by that time sunk without trace. But this initiative led to a conference of non-dramatic performing right societies, which took place at Locarno in the same year, and in which PRS participated.

Following this beginning, when in 1928 the diplomatic conference for the revision of the Berne Convention had gathered in Rome, SIAE, the Italian copyright collecting society for dramatic and non-dramatic music alike, brought together representatives of societies operating in both these fields, and from this joint conference the Confédération International des Societés d'Auteurs et Compositeurs was formed (CISAC), open to all societies operating in the field of authors rights. PRS has been a member of CISAC since its inception[13].

With the experience gained in the work and meetings of CISAC, the Society was eventually able to convince H.M. Government that it had a valuable working knowledge of the field of international copyright, and it began to be consulted more frequently by Government when topics related to this field came up for consideration. This did not necessarily mean that the two sides agreed on the issue under discussion, but at least consultations were taking place. Such an issue was the question of the monopoly position of the Society within the U.K., and its affiliates abroad. As a result of the Report from the Select Committee on the Musical Copyright Bill 1930 [14], the Board of Trade had been ordered to consider a policy to present to the next revision conference of the Berne Copyright Union on the restriction of authors' rights where they were of a monopoly nature; the whole subject was under review by a special Committee appointed by the Board of Trade, which from time to time consulted the Society [15].

It would have suited PRS very considerably if it could have persuaded a fair selection of the substantial music users who from time to time contested the size of its tariffs, as opposed to their liability to pay, to take their case to arbitration for an independent judgement. In fact on only one occasion prior to the Second World War had the Society gone to arbitration with a music user, and that was in the case of the BBC in

---

12 See Chapter 3, ante.
13 McFarlane, Copyright Collecting Societies, Grove's Dictionary of Music and Musicians, (6th ed.) (Macmillan).
14 See Chapter 8 ante.
15 Unpublished Records of the PRS.

1937. As the medium of radio was at that time the sole buyer of PRS music for broadcasting in the U.K., and therefore in a monopolist position, the income from this course was of supreme importance to the Society. Agreement between PRS and the BBC had existed almost from the commencement of broadcasting in this country, and by about 1930 about 35% of the Society's income came from this source. By 1945 the proportion had risen to nearly 50%. This arose in part because from 1929 to 1933 the BBC payments to PRS were based on a maximum percentage of revenue of 5%, but under the 1933 agreement a formula based on a sliding scale according to the number of licences issued by the BBC was adopted, which added greatly to the Society's benefit in an era of rapid growth in broadcasting licences[16] .

By 1937, the Society tried to justify a larger income from the BBC, driven by a belief in the world of music publishing that broadcasting was largely responsible for the decline in composers' royalties from the sale of sheet music and gramophone records. It was also known that the BBC under its new charter was to receive a larger share of the licence revenue and that the proportion going to the Post Office and the Treasury was to be reduced. Moreover, the BBC had started its Empire Service, and thus was making a wider use of the Society's music.

PRS offered a straight licence basis for a royalty, based on the sum of 1/- per licence, but against this the BBC offered only 5d. per licence, and declined to enter into further negotiations. In this deadlock, arbitration was the only answer, and so the case came on. Unfortunately there is no report of it. The decision was that kind of judicially imposed compromise which was later to characterise so many of the decisions of the Performing Right Tribunal: an award of 7d. per licence to the PRS in respect of Home broadcasting stations. As a result the gross annual distribution per PRS member jumped from about £242 in 1936 to about £342 in 1937[17].

There was a curious feature of negotiations between PRS and the BBC when the 1929 licence had been thrashed out. Reference has been made to the BBC's ban on microphone announcements by band-leaders to combat the abuse of song-plugging[18] . The popular publishers who had rejoined the Society in 1926 resented this, and exerted pressure on PRS to make it a condition of the licence to the BBC that this announcing ban be dropped. By virtue of its constitution the BBC was obliged to resist attempts to control its production policies, and the Corporation indicated that, not only would it take legal action on the matter, but that it would

---

16 Economists' Advisory Group,op.cit.,p.51
17 Economists Advisory Group,op.cit.,p.172
18 See Chapter 8 ante.

press the Board of Trade for an enquiry. Any such reference to that Department of State on an allegation that it had misused its monopoly powers was the last thing the Society wanted at that time, and perhaps fortunately for both sides the matter did not come to a head, as the ban was dropped, apparently due to public demand for its lifting, rather than the effect of PRS pressure[19].

War in 1939 brought an abrupt halt to the expansion of PRS, for an international copyright licensing business contributed little to the war effort. The existing rights nevertheless continued in force, and collection and distribution in respect of licences existing at the outbreak of hostilities were in general carried on with a skeleton staff.

But problems of copyright administration arose out of the fact of war itself. With the rise of the Nazi party in Germany in the early thirties, a steady trickle of Jewish and other refugees began to find their way out of Europe to Britain. More came with the annexation of Austria, and by the time of the invasion of Poland, that trickle had swelled into a flood. They numbered in their ranks many of the leading composers, lyric authors and music publishers of those countries, some of whom arrived in Britain utterly destitute.

Before Hitler's advent, GEMA had for many years been the German equivalent of PRS, and had earned a high reputation. But in 1933 it was taken under the authority of the Nazi party, and its name changed to STAGMA. In Austria a collecting society known as AKM had been founded as long ago as 1897, but when the Nazi regime occupied Austria, AKM was forcibly dissolved, and its membership obliged to join STAGMA, the operations of which were extended to Austria[20].

The foreign writers and publishers who had come to Britain had previously joined their collecting societies in their own countries, and had at that time assigned control of their works to such societies as GEMA and STAGMA in the normal way. It had been established as a rule by CISAC, the international organisation controlling authors societies, that no individual can belong to more then one national collecting society. Some emigrants claimed that as they had been deprived of their membership rights by anti-Jewish and other discriminatory legislation, to say nothing of being obliged to flee their homelands to save their lives, they were entitled to regard their membership of their native societies as annulled; they argued that they were thus able to vest their performing rights in whichever society would grant them rights of membership. Against that, at least until the

---

19 Report of the Select Committee on the Musical Copyright Bill 1930, Appendix XI pp.326/7

20 McFarlane, Copyright Collecting Societies, Grove's Dictionary of Music and Musicians, (6th edn.)(Macmillan).

outbreak of hostilities, STAGMA claimed that the performing rights of its erstwhile members who had emigrated remained vested in it. These emigrants were not able to bring their documents of title with them, and often they were involved in intricate questions of nationality and statelessness. Further, the attitudes of different societies throughout the world conflicted. The complex legal situation was rendered tragic by the desperate necessity of many of the emigrants[21].

The *Patents, Designs and Trademarks (Emergency) Legislation Act 1939* did not cover the situation, nor was it appropriate for these copyrights to vest in the Custodian of Enemy Property under the Trading with the Enemy legislation, for these people were not enemies. PRS eventually took the view that the emigrants had a right to transfer their memberships from one society to another, thus incidentally acquiring a large and important repertoire of important works for itself. As the German society continued for some years after the war under Allied supervision, it was not in a position to contest the PRS decision[22].

Although a large number of outlets for musical entertainment were closed by the war, some new types of market did open up, and agreements were made with some Government departments which to a certain extent did replace lost business. For example, an agreement was made in 1940 with ENSA (Enertainments National Service Association.) granting a global licence in respect of all entertainments provided by that organisation. Similar agreements were made with the War Office for entertainment of the home forces, and with the Ministry of Supply for entertainments for workers in Royal Ordinance Factories[23].

The cases of Ernest Turner Electrical Instruments Ltd. and Gillette Industries Ltd. against the Performing Right Society over the issue of the new programme "Music While You Work" have already been described[24]. After its inception the popularity of the programme spread very rapidly, and by 1944 it was said to be heard in 8,000 factories employing over 4½ million people. Nor was the home audience confined to factories, for by the end of the war either by radio or some form of relay PRS music was being heard in "Air raid shelters, rest centres, . . . factory canteens, workers hostels, village halls and public parks and in camps and on remote battery sites"[25]. As a result of all this, the

---

21 Unpublished Records of the PRS.
22 McFarlane, Copyright Collecting Societies, Grove's Dictionary of Music and Musicians, (6th edn.) (Macmillan).
23 Unpublished Records of the PRS.
24 See Chapter 9 ante.
25 R.A. Butler as he then was, to the PRS Annual Luncheon 1944, cited by C.F. James, op.cit.,p.103.

receipts of the Society did not fall as perhaps might have been expected on account of the war, and these new outlets very largely remained after its termination, at least in so far as a vast new audience of casual listeners to music had acquired a taste for instant entertainment in this way. Here was a public conditioned to the rapid post-war spread of popular music as a background to many forms of amusement and even working activities.

By the outbreak of war, the international association of authors' societies, CISAC, was already well established in Paris, and through its offices the international system of sophisticated accounting between one society and another was supervised. Hostilities had brought these activities to a halt, but before the surrender of France, CISAC had managed to open an office in Berne on the neutral territory of Switzerland, later transferring to Lausanne. The offices of the International Copyright Union (now WIPO) continued to operate in Switzerland throughout the war, and through these two organisations certain of the authors' societies managed to keep in touch, while putting credit balances for affiliated societies onto deposit for the duration of hostilities.

When the war in both Europe and Asia had come to an end, the problem facing the international accounting system was perhaps as formidable as in any other area of commerce. So much depended on documents of title, many of which had been destroyed. In the war-torn countries of central Europe, most of the premises in which documents had been housed had been bombed or burnt out, while a substantial proportion of copyright owners had been killed or driven to emigration. The Nazi controlled societies in Germany and Austria had to be replaced, and there was a chronic shortage of experienced staff. Against this background the 14th International Congress of CISAC was held in London in 1947. This part of the narrative is taken up again in the chapter on monopolies[26].

In 1947 also the BBC had re-introduced its television service, which before the war had simply been a limited transmission to a few hundred homes in the London area, and of no significance as far as the Society was concerned. In November 1949 a nationwide service was announced under a five-year plan. Opinion on whether the medium would supersede sound broadcasting was divided. For example, Leslie Boosey, then Chairman of PRS said, "I doubt it myself . . . it is much more costly than sound broadcasting. You can't turn it on and leave it to its own devices"[27].

---

26 See Chapter 12 post..
27 PRS Annual Luncheon 1948

Receivers were costly, hours of transmission limited, and more undivided attention was required than for radio and the gramophone. In 1947 there were 10,712,970 sound only licences and 7,467 television licences, but by 1951 there were 11,626,498 sound only licences and 586,601 television licences. While this represented a slower increase for the first five years of television than had been the case for radio in the 1920's, as the number of viewers grew, so the price of sets began to fall, and by 1956/7 there were as many people watching television as were listening to wireless [28].

With the introduction of commercial television following the *Independent Television Act 1955*, licence figures rose rapidly with the choice of programme. This growth produced increased income for the Society, though its appetite was perhaps not fully satisfied. While television expanded, its impact was felt most keenly by the cinema, and the fall in audiences began to contrast alarmingly from the proprietors' point of view with the freak record attendances of the post-war years [29].

The growth in demand for musical composition was reflected in the ever increasing number of licences issued by the Society for public performance in the true sense of the term, that is, other than by broadcasting. This would include the dance halls and public houses, concert-halls and ice rinks. Interesting statistics appear from time to time in the Society's house magazine which it issued annually or bi-annually to its members; latterly it was published under the title "Performing Right", but for the first few decades of its existence it appeared simply under the title "The PR Gazette".

Thus in 1924 the Society issued 5487 licences for the public performance of music. In the 1930's calculations were carried out by the new business department of PRS which indicated that saturation point for its licensing activities in the U.K. lay between 48,000 and 50,000 licences. By 1938 the number of licences issued had risen to 41,000, but by the mid-sixties the old calculations had been left far behind and licences in force had risen to 100,000 [30].

No doubt a substantial part of this rise is accounted for by more effective policing of infringements by the Society's staff, coupled with a greater acceptance of its claims as they became better known. At the same time the kinds of performance and the types of outlet have multiplied beyond pre-war expectations, for example with background music and juke-boxes. "No one need nowadays fear the agony of

28 Economists' Advisory Group,op.cit.,p. 82
29 P.E.P., The British Film Industry, London 1952,p.290
30 Ford, "The Composer's Expanding Market" (Performing Right), (October 1965)

complete silence''[31]. This contrasts with the view of Atkin J., who, it will be recalled, on being told in evidence by a cinema pianist at Epsom in the days of silent films that she did not know the music of the latest popular melody, and had never heard it played through, observed, "They must be very fortunate people down at Epsom"[32]. The case was that of *PRS v. Thompson*.

Technical developments were not confined to broadcasting. Although extremely popular, the 78 r.p.m. shellac record of 10 or 12 inches had never proved an entirely satisfactory means of sound reproduction. A certain jerkiness was always present, the playing quality deteriorated quickly, and the need to encapsulate a performance in at most three minutes playing time inhibited both classical and jazz recordings. It probably governed also the length of lyrics required for popular dance tunes. Accordingly attempts were made to increase the playing time of records at an early stage in the industry's history. Neophone in Britain was trying as long ago as 1904, and RCA Victor was experimenting in America in 1931.

Not until 1944 did the research of the CBS team begin in America which was to lead to the commercial exploitation of the first 33½ r.p.m. in 1948. It proved an immediate success, and unlike earlier technical developments in records[33], "the long-playing record as a commercial proposition was the practical fulfilment of a long expectation rather than a novelty"[34]. It was unfortunate for the record industry that in the same year the Victor Record Company issued a 45 r.p.m. extended play record, which as the 'single' has enjoyed some popularity ever since. Goodwill was lost with consumers in those early days as a result of the varied speed requirements calling for different sound reproducing equipment, until in the 1950's the manufacture of record players with twin pick-up heads and three speed gears solved the problem of the variety of records on the market[35]. The long playing record and the extended play record between them produced a vast boost in record sales during the fifties, once the harmonisation of equipment had been achieved, and accounted for a great increase in the number of public performances. In particular the extended play record lent itself to adaption to the juke-box[36].

31 E. D. Mackerness, A Social History of English Music, (London 1964) p.213.
32 (1918) 34 T.L.R.@352
33 See Chapter 5 ante.
34 A. Robertson, "A New Age in Recorded Music", Musical Times, May 1953.
35 There has recently been a similar consumer resistance to quadrophonic sound, in view of the heavy cost of equipment and the need to re-stock the record library.
36 Economists Advisory Group,op.cit.,p.76.

Following further research into sound frequencies, the stereo record became a commercial reality in 1953, and retail sales of reel to reel recorded tapes commenced in 1956. The magnetic tape recorder had been invented as long ago as 1899 by Vladimar Poulsen, but it did not become a commercial proposition until the development of electronic amplifiers. Despite this delay, the tape-recorder was to influence significantly the structure of the record industry[37].

In 1939 the British record industry was dominated by only three manufacturers. By 1970 there were eight large manufacturers and between 50 and 60 smaller ones. The smaller manufacturers owed much to the tape-recorder, which allowed the recording of a number of sessions of short duration, which in turn were edited to produce a master version of the best of these tape-recordings.

Faulty bars could be erased with the result that nowadays "many recordings are mosaics to a greater or lesser degree"[38].

By cutting down the high capital requirements needed to set up in record production, the tape recorder lowered the costs of entry to the industry. Previously all recording had taken place in a studio directly onto a wax disc or matrix, which could not be effectively edited, and from which all subsequent copies were made. Any errors and extraneous noise were either permanently inscribed on the matrix, or else it had to be completely re-made. The early Gennet recording studios in Richmond, Indiana, were in a warehouse beside a remote railway siding. Not surprisingly, "when freight trains passed on these tracks, all recording activity ceased"[39].

These technical developments swelled still further the record market and the outlets for musical performance. Small pop groups wrote their own material and recorded it on tape, creating small record companies to market their products. At the same time the music industry succeeded in creating in the late 1950's a record market especially for teenage demand. In the next decade British popular music staged a break-through, and rolled back the tide of American domination. By March 1964 American advance sales for the Beatles "Can't Buy Me Love" were two million, and by the following month the Beatles held not only the first five places in the American Top 100, but also the first two places in the LP charts. "It was the first time that any country had fought back against America's domination of twentieth century mass culture since

37 L. G. Wood, The Growth and Development of the Recording Industry, The Gramophone 1971,p.801.
38 A. Milner, "Music and the Radio", in Twentieth Century Music, edited by R.H.Myers (London 1968).
39 Keepnews and Grauer, A Pictorial History of Jazz,(London 1958),p.97.

the first craze for Alexander's Ragtime Band in 1912. And the irony of it was, of course, that America's rout had been achieved with what were almost entirely her own weapons''[40].

The effect on the business was dramatic. By 1961 distribution to members totalled over £2,000,000, and by 1970 receipts from collections in the U.K. and receipts from affiliates abroad had reached a total of over £6,000,000. The balance of payments between PRS and affiliated societies abroad in 1970 showed a heavy credit in favour of the British Society. Of 37 affiliates listed, PRS enjoyed a credit balance with no fewer than 27, and where any defecit existed, it was generally accounted for by exchange control restrictions. For example, while £133,695 was received from Australia and New Zealand in 1970 in respect of PRS music, only £9,126 was allocated by PRS in respect of music controlled by the Australasian society. For France the figures were £396,502 as against £184,487, while for West Germany they were £390,005 as against £89,897[41].

At the turn of the century the size of the composer's audience was limited by the physical extent of the concert hall, theatre or music hall. Both the record and the film were invented prior to the First World war, but neither were fully exploited until a later date; while they increased the demand for musical composition, the fragmented nature of the audience remained unaltered. In the 1920s, radio was the first of the media to break down the barriers to mass communication. Television later added the visual image, but both radio and television were restricted by the range of their transmitters. The launching of the Russian Sputnik heralded the breakthrough to world-wide broadcasting, for from it was developed the first communications satellite launched in 1966. Now earth-to-earth transmissions via satellite enable the composer to reach a global audience[42].

There were also far-reaching developments on the front of international copyright after 1945, in which PRS and her affiliates abroad were vitally concerned, for the performing right in the international conventions is the corner-stone of the scheme under which the international accounting and collection takes place. Until 1886 there had been no multilateral convention governing copyright relations on an international scale; prior to that date there had been a series of bilateral arrangements between various countries. But in 1858 a congress of authors and artists meeting at Brussels had called for international

---

40 C. Booker,"The Neophiliacs",(London 1969),p.38.
41 PRS Report and Accounts for 1970.
42 Economists Advisory Group,op.cit.,p.87.

regulation of authors' copyright, regardless of reciprocity, and not depending on any formality other than required in the country of first publication. The International Copyright Association was formed as a result of literary and artistic Congresses which had met at the Paris Exposition of 1878, and an unofficial conference was held at Berne in 1883, with continuation meetings in subsequent years. The work culminated in a final conference in 1886, as a result of which the Berne Convention came into being, ratified in the main by powerful Western European states, rich in intellectual talent and published works, which drew their colonies in behind them[43].

By this first convention, authors in any member country were to enjoy in any other member country the rights granted there to natives, and the term of protection was to be life plus fifty years. If however particular member states did not adopt this term, protection was to be regulated by the law of the country where protection was claimed. Revisions of the Convention have taken place at fairly frequent intervals, and gradually the scope and extent of protection has been increased. A number of minor international copyright conventions also came into being, largely in Central and Southern American states, and are known collectively as the Pan-American Conventions, but the U.K. is not a party to any of them.

Despite the development of the Berne Union, the U.S.A. and Russia had always remained outside it, in the case of the latter, in Czarist times equally as after the Revolution. But after the last war, in a new spirit of internationalism, it had been felt that there were greater chances of inducing at least the United States to subscribe to the new system. Soon after UNESCO was set up it began to interest itself in copyright affairs, and from an early stage it had begun to work towards the introduction of a new convention with a lower level of protection than Berne, but which would attract wide support. As a result the Universal Copyright Convention came into being in 1952, to which the U.S. adhered, and more recently the U.S.S.R. But apart from very considerable differences between the two standards of protection, the Berne treaty sets out in minute detail the extent of protection, giving a minimum term of post-mortem protection of fifty years, while the U.C.C. simply sketches out the extent of its protection in broad strokes, and gives a minimum term of twenty-five years[44].

---

43 McFarlane, "Copyright Conventions", Journal of the Chartered Institute of Patent Agents, April 1972,p.261.
44 McFarlane, supra.p.263.

Membership of these two major treaties extends to a very large number of the nations of the world, both developed and developing. Often the developing countries have inherited their copyright laws and convention membership from the retiring imperial power. Almost invariably the countries having the greatest number of copyright owners are developed, and they make up the copyright exporting states. The developing countries on the other hand have very few copyright owners, and as consumers of literary and musical works, and in particular educational material, they are substantially copyright importing countries[45]. Particularly in the areas of popular music and technical textbooks, certain countries enjoy virtually a monopoly position as exporters; in those countries, so far as music is concerned, the collecting societies enjoy a further monopoly.

Newly independent countries frequently were anxious to break with laws which had been enacted for them, with a built-in bias towards the imperial power and its copyright owners; in the sixties tendency developed in the emerging countries to reduce copyright protection in their national laws. In response to the general feelings of dissatisfaction in certain groups of countries, two important study meetings were held to examine closely the problems which copyright presented for them. and to attempt to formulate general principles which they could incorporate when drafting their own national legislation. One was designed for African states, and held at Brazzaville in 1963, as a result of which a Draft African Model Copyright Law was produced with precedents for pruning back the high standards of copyright protection set by the developed countries. A similar meeting for East Asian countries was held at New Delhi in 1967, just before the now notorious Stockholm Conference for the revision of the Berne Convention[46].

At the revision conference the interested groups were no doubt too unyielding in the stands they adopted, and a spirit of real compromise was not in evidence. Many developing countries were anxious to continue their adherence to the high level Berne Convention, or in certain cases to join it. At the same time, they wanted to enjoy considerable relaxations of the Convention requirements so long as they remained in a state of development. So to the new text of the Berne Convention as revised at Stockholm there was added a Protocol regarding Developing Countries. It was to be an integral part of the new

---

45 McFarlane, "International Copyright-The Crisis Resolved?" 1971 Solicitors Journal,p.651.
46 McFarlane, supra,p.651.

revised text, and any country adopting the Stockholm draft had also to adopt the Protocol.

The provisions of the Protocol were not attractive to copyright exporting countries. They gave developing countries the right to reduce the period of copyright protection by up to 25 years, a drastic cutting back of the rights of translation, and considerable increases in exemption from copyright in favour of educators, broadcasters and other users. Not surprisingly, the countries representing copyright owners soon made it clear that they were not going to accede to either the Protocol or the substantive provisions of the revised text that went with it, for "That the developing countries are entitled to cultural as well as economic aid is not generally disputed, but it would not be right to envisage the furnishing of the former solely at the expense of authors and publishers[47].

Deadlock resulted, as the developed countries, homes of the leading authors' societies, resolutely refused to accept the Stockholm Protocol and the substantive provisions of the revised text; ominous rumblings from the developing countries hinted that they might withdraw from Berne and with other states in their category set up a new low standard convention to meet their special needs. That this should be avoided was of crucial importance to musical performing rights just as much as to literary interests in the developed countries. Already some domestic laws re-enacted by newly independent states which had formerly been colonies had deprived non-national composers of performing rights. If the trend were to spread much further, the whole system of international copyright and affiliated copyright collecting societies could collapse.

Just as the stalemate seemed to be hardening into a permanence, the influence of mediators began to yield results. A joint study group was established to look into the whole field of international copyright, and to seek a way out of the impasse. This called for both the Berne Convention and the U.C.C. to be revised at conferences which were to be held at the same time and at the same place.

The group recommended that (1) Article XVII of the U.C.C. (the Safeguard Clause) should be removed in the case of developing countries, (2) certain rights not previously in the U.C.C. should be written into that convention, and, (3) less extensive concessions to developing countries should be made in both conventions. Preparatory meetings were held in the following months, and eventually on 5th July 1971 the conference for the revision of both the Berne and the Universal copyright conventions

---

47 R. F.Whale, Copyright,p.182.

began in Paris. The revised texts of both conventions were signed at the same place on 24th July, just over four years after the closure of the ill-fated Stockholm Conference. As a result, the Stockholm Protocol was finally laid to rest, and the valuable revisions to the text of the Berne Convention which were worked out in Stockholm in 1967 have largely been incorporated in the Paris Revision.

The kernel of concessions to developing countries is the preferential treatment given them in the areas of translation and reproduction, which introduces effectively the same system in both conventions. A scheme of compulsory licences has been erected for both translation rights and reproduction rights, representing considerable concessions by both sides. In practice these rules have set up the border lines within which negotiations between copyright owner and copyright user can take place. If experience shows it necessary to resort to compulsory licences to any appreciable extent, the schemes worked out in Paris will be that much less successful[48].

Thus the authors' societies were brought back from the brink of what for them would have been unmitigated disaster. If the developing countries' new habit of striking out the performing right in their domestic copyright laws for non-partial composers had spread, then the operations of the authors' societies and their agents in those territories would have been effectively terminated. At best the system of international collecting and accounting would only have carried on as between the European states, America and the English speaking dominions. But this threat has now receded, at least for the time being.

The international system received a new stimulus in 1973 with the accession of the Soviet Union to the U.C.C., for that country also intends to set up monopoly organisations to exploit the international copyright system to her own advantage. Some commentators suggested that the motive behind this move was to extend Soviet control over manuscripts written in the Soviet Union and sent abroad for publication[49]. But even if this is partially right, it is not the only intention. Already a Soviet copyright agency has been established which has entered into an agreement with PRS to pay £39,000 in sterling in respect of royalties for live performances in the Soviet Union of PRS works, retrospective to Russian accession to the Universal Copyright Convention[50]. This estimate may, according to latest reports, prove to be too optimistic, as under copyright

---

48 McFarlane, "International Copyright: The Crisis Resolved?", 1972 Solicitors Journal, p.652.
49 H. Bloom, "The end of Samizdat?"
50 Daily Telegraph, 21st June 1974, p.6.

law in the U.S.S.R. payment can only be made in respect of live performances, for example at concerts, variety shows and in hotels; there is no royalty entitlement in respect of performances in the course of films, the playing of records, or during broadcasts[51].

51 Performing Right, November 1974,p.6.

12
Monopolistic Aspects of the Performing Right Society

Copyright, and in particular the exercise of the performing right in the music industry, has come under close scrutiny in recent years as governments have concerned themselves more and more with monopoly situations in the private sector. The anti-cartel articles in the *Treaty of Rome* have caused a minute inspection of the business practices and operations of GEMA, the German performing right society, and the decision, to be examined in this chapter, has the widest implications for the authors' societies as at present constituted. But the problem is by no means a fresh one, for there is evidence that at the earliest known date of the exercise of a performing right on behalf of right owners by a single representative collecting society in this country, the Executive had already marked it down as a monopoly situation.

Thus when the Secretary of the Dramatic Authors Society gave evidence to the Copyright Commission 1875/6[1], on the manner in which the performing right in literary and dramatic works was exercised by his organisation at that time, he mentioned that on its behalf he had applied for permission to be registered under the *Friendly Societies Act 1875* in order that the Society could sue in its own name for infringements. But in response to the application he had received the following reply from the Lords Commissioners of the Treasury[2]. "Their Lordships desire me to inform you that they are unable to comply with your request inasmuch as it appears to them that the purposes of the Dramatic Authors Society are sufficiently in restraint of trade to be capable of being registered under the Trades Union Act 1871, and a portion under the Amendment Act lately passed."

Again, when the Society was set up, in the first cases on liability which it brought, it was met with the defence that the operation carried on was that of a combination for imposing restrictive conditions on the conduct of a trade or business, in effect an unlawful combination by

---

1 See Chapter 4 ante.
2 Copyright Commission 1875/6, Minutes of Evidence, p.121.

virtue of some of its objects being in restraint of trade. Fortunately for the Society it was held that PRS was not such an unlawful combination, but the shots, though wide, were sufficiently close to the target to cause serious embarrassment. The monopolistic aspects of the enterprise could not be concealed, and Government was keeping an eye on the situation[3].

By 1935 in approving of the aims of the Society, and of its existence, the qualification was being made that "If such an association is to function effectively, it must obtain as near a super-monopoly as is possible of the monopolies conferred upon composers by the Copyright Acts"[4]. The suggestion was there made that where an association controlled the rights, there should be an opportunity for the music user to appeal to arbitration or to some other tribunal[5].

From 1930 onwards the question of Governmental freedom to deal with any abuse of copyright monopoly rights in the U.K. was being considered inside the then Board of Trade[6]. That it was not raised at an earlier date was due to postponement of the next revision of the Berne Convention by the Second World War. Meanwhile the Canadians set up their Copyright Appeal Board, and thus became the first such organisation specifically designed to control monopolistic aspects of copyright[7].

In America the American Society of Composers, Authors and Publishers had been founded in 1914, the same year as PRS, and it developed very rapidly. The scope for expansion of a collecting society in America was enormous, for although the territory to be covered was large, communications in the United States were highly developed, and the population was evenly spread through many sizeable towns, so that collection of royalties was a practical economic proposition. The rapid spread of popular music which followed the closing of Storyville and the departure of the coloured musicians from New Orleans[8], was soon to be linked to the introduction of broadcasting. Within a year of the commencement of the new medium, over 500 broadcasting stations were operating in the United States. ASCAP built up an immense repertoire, and in many countries the ASCAP repertoire was more frequently performed than that held by the national society[9].

---

3 See e.g. PRS v. Edinburgh Magistrates, 1922 S.C.165.
4 Report of the Select Committee on the Musical Copyright Bill 1930.
5 See Chapter 8 ante.
6 Economists Advisory Group,op.cit.,p.50.
7 See Chapter 8 ante.
8 Rex Harris, "Jazz", (Pelican 4th edn.)p.94 et seq..
9 Unpublished Records of PRS.

Although anti-monopoly or anti-trust laws are now becoming familiar to European lawyers, the development of a sophisticated anti-trust system began in the United States. Its roots lay in the deflation which acted on that country's extraordinary expansion during the mid-nineteenth century. Businessmen were driven towards organising their affairs in monopolies or trusts which acted to the detriment of the independent farmers and small businessmen. Agitation from these factions in their turn produced the first contra-monopoly legislation in the *Sherman Anti-Trust Act 1890*, with wide powers to break up cartels.

The Sherman Act, as amended[10], empowered the Department of Justice in its civil jurisdiction to authorise the several district attorneys to institute proceedings in equity to restrain violations of the Act. On its criminal side its powers are very wide, providing that violators of the code may on conviction be fined up to a maximum of 50,000 dollars or imprisonment for up to one year, or both[11]. In cases under investigation, the Department of Justice carries on investigations to determine whether to institute criminal or civil proceedings, and within the Department there is an anti-trust division policing the anti-trust laws, and handling and processing complaints which may emanate from private parties. It ensures that district court decrees in government cases are enforced, and if there are violations, the Department may secure a contempt citation[12].

A feature of the machinery is that very often an organisation under investigation will submit to a consent decree to avoid a published judgement and any unfavourable publicity. This has the effect that frequently disgruntled defendants after the event grumble that if they had not submitted, but had gone to a contest in court, they might have obtained far more lenient treatment.

As had the Society in Britain, ASCAP built up its early operation on a basis of blanket licences, and with the advent of commercial radio in the U.S., looked forward to a new and substantial source of revenue. The broadcasters were engaged in interstate commerce, and they persuaded the American government that the combination of copyright in owners in the shape of ASCAP unreasonably restrained trade. The principle of blanket licensing as such was not in issue, merely the question of whether a broadcaster who wished to keep logs of music used on each of his programmes could insist on an ASCAP licence based on the extent of his use of ASCAP music.

---

10 26 Stat.209(1890), as amended by 36 Stat.1167(1911), and 15 U.S.C. Sec.4(1952).
11 Ss.1&2,26 Stat.209(1890), as amended by 50 Stat.693(1937) and 15 U.S.C. Secs.1&2 as amended by July 7 1955, Public Law 135, 84th Cong.1st Sess.
12 Joseph Taubman, Copyright and Anti-trust Law(New York 1960)p.120.

In 1941 the Department of Justice took action against ASCAP, which speedily submitted to a consent decree in which no evidence was taken, and no judgement given on the facts. Although it was a condition that ASCAP was taken not to have infringed any law, that society undertook inter alia not to license the public performance for profit of any musical work except on the basis, so far as network broadcasting is concerned. that the issue of a single licence fixing a single royalty for that performance by network radio should permit the simultaneous broadcasting of that performance by all stations on the network broadcasting such performance, without the necessity of separate licences for each station[13].

There still remained the issue of whether the collective determination of a rate for the use of the ASCAP repertoire by negotiations between that society and such national music users as the broadcasting industry and the hotel industry amounted to price-fixing[14]. This was solved by an amendment to the consent decree on March 14th, 1950, which empowered any music user to apply to the Federal Court for a determination of the rate to be paid by him to ASCAP[15]. There have been several rate fixing hearings based on these amendments, and the most recent alteration to the decree was on 7th January 1960[16].

From the early days of radio ASCAP found itself in conflict with the broadcasting interests, which throughout the thirties resisted, so far as they were able, all attempts to license them. Eventually ASCAP succeeded in setting up a licensing procedure for them, but they accepted the terms with considerable reluctance, and when in 1940 ASCAP sought to introduce new licensing terms, the members of the National Association of Broadcasters decided to boycott ASCAP music by using music in the public domain, and by arranging for new music to be composed which would not pass into the ASCAP net. It will be recalled that the infant PRS had been faced with a similar threat rather earlier in its existence, when in about 1919 the British Music Union Limited advertised a catalogue of so-called free music which was either out of copyright or in which the performing right was not asserted[17]. This attempt was a total failure, and ASCAP confidently anticipated that the American broadcasters would have no better luck.

---

13 Consent decree in Civ.13-95,United States v. ASCAP was entered in the District Court for the Southern District of New York on March 4th 1941.

14 H. Finkelstein,"Practical Copyright Problems",7 Anti-trust Bulletin 728.

15 Joseph Taubman,op.cit.,p.3.

16 The decree, as so amended, is reported in CCH Trade Reg.Rep.,para.69,612,(1960).

17 See Chapter 6 ante.

In this expectation they were sadly disappointed. The broadcasters set up another licensing body to control their operation, and the boycott began. It was surprisingly successful, and involved as it was in anti-trust proceedings, ASCAP was obliged to settle its dispute with the broadcasting organisations. But the new organisation known as Broadcast Music Incorporated (BMI) has ever since remained in competition with ASCAP, so that since 1940 there has, uniquely among the major countries, ceased to be a monopoly authors' society in the United States[18]. In fact BMI was on the scene just in time to be involved in parallel anti-trust proceedings with the first ASCAP investigation, and submitted to a consent decree on 9th May 1941[19].

When in 1947 the CISAC member societies gathered in London for their first post-war Congress, there existed a feeling of cautious optimism that the steady expansion known in the years before the war would continue. It therefore came as a considerable shock to the assembled delegates when in the very first session the ASCAP delegation announced that it had been "advised" by the U.S. Department of Justice to resign from CISAC, and immediately upon making this announcement their delegation physically withdrew from the Congress[20].

As the events leading up to this had taken place in the United States during the war years, they had not attracted much attention in Europe. When the full implications were known, they excited considerable alarm among the delegates, for they saw in BMI a threat to destroy the performing right in broadcasting by the music users in effect taking over the rights of the copyright owners in a form of vertical integration. Accordingly CISAC declined initially to recognise BMI, which had to buy its way into business and acquire a repertoire by paying out to composers and publishers at high rates fixed in advance. It built up such a strong repertoire that by 1955 PRS could no longer afford to ignore it, and the two organisations concluded a contract of reciprocal representation.

At about the same time several other important authors societies came to the same conclusion, and agreed similar contracts with BMI, as a result of which the Department of Justice allowed BMI to join CISAC, and ASCAP to rejoin at the same time. For those who wished to read them however, the signs were clearly available that governments were

---

18 McFarlane, Copyright Collecting Societies, Grove's Dictionary of Music and Musicians, (6th edn.) (Macmillan).
19 Rothenberg, Copyright and Public Performance of Music,p.148, (1954)
20 Unpublished Records of PRS.

prepared to take vigorous action against the effects of the monopoly situations among authors' societies.

If the CISAC conference in 1947 had disturbed the European authors' societies, which became conscious for the first time of the significance of wartime anti-trust developments in the United States, they were allowed no time to recover. Well before the Second World War the then Board of Trade was turning its attention to the monopoly position of PRS, and preparations had been made to attack the position at the next revision conference for the Berne Convention[21]. The postponed conference eventually took place at Brussels in 1948, and as this was the first revision since 1928 considerable alteration was called for to take account of the rapid technological advances over the intervening twenty years. It was clear that in the U.K. a new copyright statute would be needed to give effect to the alterations, and that Parliamentary time must somehow be found for the instrument.

Article 11(1) Brussels Revision of the Berne Convention 1948 stated: "The authors of dramatico-musical or musical works shall enjoy the exclusive right of authorising (i) the public presentation and public performance of their works (ii) the public distribution by any means of the presentation and performance of their works . . . " But the British delegation to the Brussels revision conference bore in mind the original recommendations of 1929 that music users should have "a right of appeal to an independent body when they are faced with unreasonable demands, and are unable to come to a mutually satisfactory agreement with the Society"[22].

Accordingly the British delegation made its acceptance of Article 11 subject to the following declaration. "The United Kingdom delegation accepts the provisions of Article 11 of the Convention on the understanding that H.M. Government remains free to enact such legislation as it may consider necessary to prevent or deal with any abuse of the monopoly rights conferred upon owners of copyright by the law of the United Kingdom."

Attempts were nonetheless made by H.M. Government to reassure the society that its position was at least partly understood. A Departmental Committee set up within the then Board of Trade in 1935 to examine the proposed tribunal in the light of Britain's obligations under the Berne Convention had stated that no substantial grounds for complaint existed about the manner in which the performing right was

21 Economists Advisory Group,op.cit.,p.50.
22 Special Report, Select Committee on the Musical Copyright Bill 1930.

administered in this country; because additions were being proposed to Article 11 of the Berne Convention, it should not be taken to imply that protective legislation was in fact necessary[23].

Even after the declaration had been made at the 1948 Brussels Revision Conference, Mr. Harold Wilson as he then was, at that time President of the Board of Trade, could still tell the Society that the declaration on monopoly abuse had been made "not because there is any evidence at all of necessity for the alteration, but because it is essential to preserve the position if at some later date there should ever be legislation to control the rate of royalties. I have received as yet no such evidence. I think this Society has followed a policy for the past twenty years or so which has been in my view of the very highest national interest"[24].

Whether the officers of the Society were re-assured by that tribute is not known. But at the same time as the Government was erecting defences at the 1948 revision conference to deal with any abuses of the monopoly situation which might occur on the domestic front at a later date, a train of events had been set in motion which was soon to affeet the situation to a considerable degree.

In order to gain approval from large groups of music users in the early days of its existence, the Society had entered licence agreements with powerful organisations at rates which were sometimes purely nominal. Worse, from its own point of view, PRS failed to alter this significantly in its own favour during the inter-war period, being apprehensive of government reaction. While this did not matter so much during a period of deflation during the Twenties and Thirties with fairly constant money values, when severe inflation began during the Second World War, a number of the more important tariffs appeared quite uneconomic. When the Society tried to revise certain of these tariffs to bring them into line with post-war conditions, it ran into considerable opposition from various music users.

Some tariffs being re-negotiated in the immediate post-war period dated back to the early 1920's, and very considerable increases were needed to bring them up to what from the Society's point of view represented a reasonable return. But by the close of the 1940's forms of entertainment media such as cinema and the music hall were experiencing considerable competition from outlets in the ascendency, like television and gramophone records. Traditional entertainments like

23 Economists Advisory Group,op.cit.,p.111.
24 C. F. James,op.cit.,p.118.

the circus were declining steadily. Accordingly it was argued that the Society's tariffs should take account of changed economic circumstances for particular users [25].

Some music users were nonetheless still extremely profitable, and the Society felt that a few isolated cases of hardship such as the circus would be used by the profitable media as well to oppose PRS increases in all tariff negotiations. Those governing PRS affairs realised that they were in a difficult position. On the one hand, many tariffs were simply not compensating for the fall in the value of sterling, and appeared derisory when set against comparable tariffs operated by Continental collecting societies. On the other, the Government had indicated that it was not enamoured of the Society's monopoly position, and might move against it if there were any sign of abuse. The growing resistance among music users to its tariff revision led to a note of caution in an editorial in the Society's magazine: ". . . a Society such as ours, representing as it does almost the whole of the world's composers, cannot by reason of its very strength it holds exercise its powers in an arbitrary manner. We should not seek to be the sole judges of the value of our rights, but should agree upon this by negotiation, and if that fails we must submit the matter to arbitration" [26].

Unfortunately for the Society, no music user agreed to go to arbitration in the post-war period, and PRS was obliged to impose its new tariffs unilaterally in cases of failure in attempts to reach agreement. The music users had banded themselves together as the National Council of Music Users, and had retained Members of Parliament to represent their interests. No doubt they had reliable information of what was afoot.

In April 1951 a new Copyright Committee was appointed against a background of alterations to the Berne Convention, consumer resistance to tariff revisions, and new technical developments. When its Report comes to deal with the subject of performing rights, there is an onimous ring to the opening paragraph:" . . .we have been faced with a large amount of criticism from many quarters directed at the way in which rights of public performance are exercised. The evidence leaves us in little doubt that this criticism is not without its justification". Accordingly as a principal question the Committee set out to consider "whether the right of public performance as hitherto enjoyed and as interpreted in the courts is unreasonably wide or has been exercised in a manner prejudicial to the public interest" [27].

---

25 Economists Advisory Group,op.cit.,p.112.
26 Performing Right, (1946),p.3.
27 Cmnd. 8662,paras.122 & 123.

The chief witnesses who gave evidence before the Committee on behalf of the Society were the Chairman and the General Manager of the day, Leslie Boosey and Charles James respectively. They were well aware that the question had been referred to the Committee for its consideration of whether the recommendation of the Select Committee on the Musical Copyright Bill 1930 should be adopted, that is, whether a tribunal should be set up to which the music users could refer the PRS tariffs if agreement between them and the Society could not be reached. The Society held the view that outright opposition would be useless, and accordingly its witnesses took the line that PRS did not oppose the creation of a tribunal the function of which would be to restrain the abuse of copyright. Indeed, they submitted that there might be advantages for the Society in that tariffs fixed or endorsed by an independent body could not be reasonably called an abuse of power[28].

It was appreciated by the Copyright Committee that if he had to carry out his own collection, the individual composer could have no expectation of harvesting his own royalties from the music user, but that only through association with others was there any prospect of securing an income. Curiously, in view of the previous existence in the nineteenth century of the Dramatic Authors Society[29], the 1951 Committee observed, "So far as we are aware, there is no Society comparable to the Performing Right Society concerned with the collection of the rights of performance in dramatic works, which probably present less difficulty in enforcement than those which face composers"[30]. The Committee had received evidence from virtually every living authority on copyright in Britain, together with no fewer than 63 organisations dealing either directly or indirectly with copyright. On the Committee sat F. E. Skone-James, who had edited Copinger since 1927, and who had dominated the copyright Bar more completely than any other man this century. Yet so utterly had the Dramatic Authors Society vanished that no one was aware that it had existed. My own enquiries at the Society of Authors[31], and at the Societé des Auteurs et Compositeurs Dramatiques reveal a total absence of trace[32].

After reviewing the history and constitution of PRS, the Committee agreed that it was dealing with a body which was substantially monopolistic because practically all music publishers and popular composers

---

28 Unpublished Records of PRS.
29 See Chapter 4 ante.
30 Cmnd.8662,para.130.
31 Reply dated 11th May 1973.
32 Reply dated 1st March 1974.

were members, that all the performing rights of its members other than dramatic rights were assigned to the Society, and that in consequence it was virtually impossible for the promoters of musical entertainments generally to avoid the necessity for obtaining a PRS licence to carry out their operations[33]. It referred to criticism of the Society which had been given before it by a number of bodies, including the Music Users Federation, the Association of Ballrooms, and representatives of theatres, caterers and cinematograph exhibitors, referring apparently to the arbitrary way in which tariffs had been established, and arbitrarily allowed; also that the Society had been unwilling or unable to furnish lists of all the separate titles of works in which it claimed the performing right. When many millions of works were controlled, and these being constantly added to, the provision of such a list is clearly impossible in any complete form, and the Committee recorded that it did not regard this last complaint as being of any substance[34].

The question of tariffs it regarded as more important, but it was conceded that there was no complaint that PRS had ever declined to issue a licence for the performance of its music, and indeed both the BBC and the National Council of Social Service had stated in evidence that they had no complaint against the Society. No doubt the Corporation felt that it would derive little advantage from any other response, for the performing right as such was not going to be revoked by the new Copyright Bill, and the broadcasting authorities in this country were well aware of the PRS complaint that its music was broadcast for a return of far smaller royalties than obtained in comparable European countries.

A summary was made by the Committee of what it felt were the results of the manner in which PRS and PPL operated their respective performing rights[35]. These were (a) the establishment of varying tariffs of royalties applicable without appeal, (b) the changing of rates of royalties at short notice, and in an arbitrary manner, (c) the tariffs covered the whole range of public performances in the widest sense of the term, so that collecting societies' licences were biting on performances which many people would not regard as taking place in public and (d) the restrictions imposed by PPL in certain cases prevented the free use of copyright material even if the royalties demanded were paid.

Clearly (a), (b), and (d) foreshadowed some kind of quasi-judicial body, and it might have been expected that (c) would result in a clear re-

---

33 Cmnd.8662.para.136.
34 Cmnd.8662,para.137.
35 Cmnd.8662,para.156.

commendation that the scope of public performance as defined by the cases should be cut back, although this turned out to be only partly the case. The Committee did however recommend[36] that the performing right in gramophone records established in *Gramophone Co.Ltd. v. Stephen Carwardine & Co.*[37] should not be taken away from the manufacturers. But the sharp criticism of PPL in the Report shows that this conclusion was only reached after considerable heart-searching among the Committee members. The consideration which apparently swayed the balance was that total lack of control might make the profession of musician still less attractive, and that therefore in the long run the public might lose.

In so far as performances by broadcasts and records were concerned, the Committee suggested that all member organisations of the National Council of Social Service should be entitled to obtain limited exemption from performing right royalties[38]. This recommendation did not pass into the 1956 Act, and strictly speaking under U.K. law copyright owners are entitled to royalties for performances of their works in the course of divine worship. But on the general question of public performance by radio or gramophone in such places as hotel lounges the Committee eventually concluded that they should make no recommendation[39]. The members felt in general that in these cases the resulting performance was either an ancillary attraction to a business run for profit, or an added amenity for which those enjoying it or providing it could reasonably be expected to pay. Nevertheless there remains in some quarters unease about the wide interpretation of the scope of public performance, which manifested itself recently in *PRS v. Glasgow Rangers F.C. Supporters Club*[39a], when it was tried in Scotland at first instance.

Reference was made by the Committee to the Copyright Appeal Board which had existed in Canada since 1931[40], and approval expressed of the system which operated in that country[41]. The recommendation was that the same principle should be recognised in the United Kingdom, although no reference was made to the fact that the proposal had been put forward in this country in 1930[42]. It was not considered that the

---

36 Cmnd. 8662,para.184.
37 [1934]Ch.450.
38 Cmnd. 8662,para.194.
39 Cmnd.8662,para.196.
39a See page 134 ante.
40 Cmnd. 8662,para.207.
41 McFarlane, Copyright Collecting Societies, Grove's Dictionary of Music and Musicians, (6th edn.) (Macmillan).
42 Report of the Select Committee on the Musical Copyright Bill 1930.

application of the *Arbitration Act 1950* would be sufficient to meet the situation, and the final proposal was that the Tribunal should be set up charged with the following powers:

(a) to review and revise tariffs actually in operation, both as to the class of entertainment covered by a tariff and the fees chargeable thereunder,

(b) to make new tariffs where none existed or where the scope of any existing tariff seems to be inappropriate, and

(c) to determine whether or not refusals to grant licences (or whether any conditions attached to licences issued) were detrimental to the public interest, and if so to grant licences of right, subject to such condition as the Tribunal might decide[43].

The Report of the Copyright Committee was dated 1st July 1952, but the *Copyright Act 1956* did not come into force until 1st June 1957, having received the Royal Assent on 5th November 1956. The interim period provoked a certain amount of discussion on the merits of copyright protection, and Sir Arnold Plant, then Sir Ernest Cassel, Professor of Commerce in the University of London, took the opportunity afforded by the Stamp Memorial Lecture 1953 to attack the length and extent of protection granted under the British law at that time[44]. Professor Sir Arnold Plant himself gave evidence to the Copyright Committee, but his ideas were not accepted. It was very much an expression of an individual opinion, which if it had been adopted would have upset the comity of the international copyright conventions.

His thesis was that, far from being too short or inadequate, the protection, at least to the heirs of composers, was over generous, and that the output of musical composition would be unaffected by a reduction of the period of copyright. In the course of his lecture he examined a number of issues bearing on the performing right and the monopoly position of the copyright collecting societies.

On the other hand, he argued, the market for consumption of copyright material had changed vastly in this country since copyright privileges had first been introduced here. He put the date at some four hundred years ago, though it seems scarcely accurate to use as a base point what were merely limited licences for printers at that time. Nevertheless, the factors of change which he highlighted were:

(a) the greatly increased population, to which a producer had much greater access with improved transport,

---

43 Cmnd.8662,para.211.
44 Published by the Athlone Press as "The New Commerce in Ideas and Intellectual Property."

(b) Wider education and changed habits and tastes.

(c) greater purchasing powers,

(d) increased leisure, coupled with increased requirements for vocational training,

(e) improved artificial lighting and heating,

(f) the prolongation of the average life,

(g) new aids to declining sight and hearing in old age.[45]

These affected in Plant's view the size of the potential market for a performance or an edition. Coupled with this he pointed to other benefits of technical advance such as reduced printing costs, and the advantages of micro-photography. He referred to the effect of the recording in the multiplication of the reproduction of such perform-ances, although he seemed to ignore the fact that performances of musical works were scarcely exploited by the copyright owners in this country until the gramophone had become a commercial reality and not a toy.

Plant drew attention to the monopoly position of PRS in his day[46]. He observed that the simplification of the licensing procedure by the medium of a collecting society had gone so far as to prevent negotiation of the terms best suited to individual cases. Copyright owners, he said, might fix their own tariffs and instruct the collecting agency what terms to charge and collect. Concert promoters would then choose from a detailed list or tariff on which they could see the amount asked for each work, and assess for themselves whether they could take an expensive and popular work, or should make do with a cheaper and less popular one. By this system, argued the Professor, some copyright owners stood to gain and others to lose more than they did under the standard PRS arrangement.

But this proposal is not practical. It would be impossible for the Society to produce a complete list of the works it controlled at any point in time, and still less practical for a busy concert promoter, or any other music user such as a juke-box owner, to go through millions of works on the Society's repertoire making a selection based on competitive prices. Apart from these two factors, the administrative cost of such protracted negotiation by PRS would rise to a figure quite uneconomical for all but the most successful composers.

The result as he observes is that the division of pooled receipts between different types of composers, and between composers and publishers must be arbitrary. There is discrimination or weighting in

---

45 Plant, ''The New Commerce in Ideas and Intellectual Property'', (Athlone Press),p.6.
46 Plant, supra, p.24.

10   Part of the PRS' computer room.

favour of serious music to which the successful popular composer in Plant's view might object. That they did not, he considered to be because they have no alternative easily open to them. This is not strictly true, for there is nothing to prevent the top ten earning PRS members withdrawing and setting up their own licensing body; this would be able to carry out its functions for a much lower administrative cost than the Society now does.

At present it is thought that under the current system the Society is obliged to license and collect on behalf of 80% of its membership which accounts for no more than 20% of the total income. The most obvious barrier is the transience of success in the world of popular music, but both among composers and publishers there appears to be in the last analysis a feeling that the weaker members must be subsidised. But the evidence given to the Copyright Committee enabled Professor Plant to draw the conclusion that PRS operated a discriminatory monopoly just as do most public utility corporations such as gas, electricity and water suppliers, and differed from them only in that its tariffs were not at that time subject to the control of a public authority. Plant at least did not find it surprising that the Copyright Committee had recommended that the tariffs or organisations such as the Society should be subject to independent review[47].

He also dealt with the performing right in gramophone records, but did not bear as harshly with the manufacturers and their change of attitude between 1909 and 1933 as had the Copyright Committee. In his view the manufacturers' interest was only to augment their income by the exploitation of the performing right; the suppression as such came from the performers in the shape of the Musicians Union. To remove this interest in his view was the real reason for nullifying the Carwardine case[48].

Perhaps the most interesting conclusion he reaches is that if society wishes to confer special privileges on authors, composers and artists, there is a more satisfactory method than granting an extended period of post-mortem protection, which simply extends to the benefit of the heirs of the publisher assignee. As the financial rewards to an author in the form of royalties for a successful work are often compressed into a very short period after publication, and therefore subject to very high rates of income tax, with only a small allowance for spreadover, he seemed to suggest that a scheme for equalisation of earnings for authors and

---

47 Plant,op.cit.,p.25.
48 Plant,op.cit.,p.29.

consequently lower rates of taxation in their successful years would be more beneficial[49].

Although there are only very bare provisions of this kind in the law of the U.K., Ireland adopted an even more extensive scheme than Plant's suggestion in *S.2 Finance Act 1969 (Ireland)*. By this, special relief from income tax is given in respect of earnings derived from certain works of ''cultural or artistic merit''. The work must be an original creative work, either book, musical composition, play, painting or sculpture, and the taxpayer must establish residence in Ireland. The concession extends to performing right royalties, and may be a fiscal technique increasingly used by low population countries with high cultural standards, which are interested in attracting international names permanently to their shores. There is a considerable gain in international prestige at the cost of only a very small loss to the Revenue.

Almost inevitably a Tribunal was set up under *S.23 Copyright Act 1956*, known as the Performing Right Tribunal; it enjoys jurisdiction over three types of right only. Firstly, what may loosely be called the performing right in literary, dramatic or musical works; secondly, the right to cause a sound recording to be heard in public or to be broadcast, and thirdly, the right to cause a television broadcast to be seen or heard in public. The new copyright in broadcast programmes was itself one of the innovations introduced in the 1956 Act as a result of the deliberations of the Copyright Committee. The function of the Tribunal is, on the one hand, to confirm or vary licence schemes being operated by licensing organisations and, on the other, to adjudicate on complaints by prospective licensees aggrieved by the refusal of a licensing organisation to grant them a licence. So far most of the cases have concerned confirmation or variation of existing schemes under the first head.

The judgements of the Tribunal are not published as such in any recognised series of reports[50]. The Tribunal sits on a part-time basis, and less than a score of judgements have been given since its inception. Generally PRS has been the licensing body involved, although Phonographic Performance was on one occasion concerned. Two recent cases have involved the same adversaries, the BBC and PRS, the first case taking place in 1967, the second in 1972. The services of the Performing Right Tribunal are being called upon ever less frequently; this has been the experience in other fields where Tribunals set up to

---

49 Plant,op.cit.,p.13.
50 They are available in typescript from the Secretary of the Tribunal.

provide a cheap and accessible forum have not received the rate of work originally estimated.

There has been very little consideration of law in the decided cases; the common thread running through them is of the Tribunal members trying hard to come to terms with what they apparently regard as the "commodity" of copyright. In the result they have tended to treat the litigants as vendor and consumer respectively of that commodity. Thus in *Theatres National Committee v.* PRS (PRT 20/26) it was said in the course of the judgement, "The actual figure at which the Tribunal have arrived has been reached by having regard to two guide-posts pointing to what a willing buyer would pay to a willing seller on a free market." Again, in *PRS v. Cinematograph Exhibitors Association of Great Britain and Ireland* (PRT 21/66), the Tribunal chairman stated that one of the tests for a tribunal should be the application, so far as the evidence allowed them so to do, of a "willing buyer/willing seller test", in which price constituted an important element.

All too often the Tribunal has been faced with a mere rate-fixing exercise, after negotiations have left a gap between the price one side is prepared to offer and that which the other side is disposed to pay. In such circumstances it is not altogether surprising that a Tribunal composed of commercial men drawn from outside the copyright world should have sought to strike a balance between buyer and seller on a free market basis. But this test appealed to the music users apparently no more than to PRS, which by their submissions both sides made clear that they required a proper evaluation of the 'worth' of the music, having regard to the peculiarities of the area of the entertainment industry currently under examination. It cannot be said that the Tribunal has often acted with conspicuous boldness, for in general its decision has simply divided the difference between the two parties.

On the other side of the coin, the existence of the Tribunal does stifle the kind of criticism which was made to the 1951 Copyright Committee by the aggrieved music users. Particularly so in the case of Phonographic Performance Limited, which was extremely fortunate to escape from the Committee's deliberations without a direct recommendation that its rights should be cut back, the source of grievance has been removed, in so far as any refusal to grant a licence can be met with prompt reference to the Tribunal. In practice the policy of PPL on this point has been effectively reversed by the Tribunal's existence, without any need to take a complaint to it. It is arguable however whether the music users obtain their "commodity" any more cheaply than before.

At the same time as the Performing Right Tribunal was coming into existence in the U.K., the European Economic Community was being set up by the *Treaty of Rome 1957*. The aim of the so-called Common

177

Market, as expressed in Article 2 of the Treaty, is to promote in the member states "a harmonious development of economic activities, a continuous and balanced expansion, an increase in stability, an accelerated raising of the standard of living and closer relations between the states belonging to it."

More particularly this means the free movement of goods and capital and labour; elimination of customs duties between member states and the setting up of a common tariff, a common agricultural policy, and a community transport system relating to transit. But there are also stringent rules on questions of competition and unfair trading relating to abuse of a dominant position. The copyright collecting societies were to discover that these would be applied by the Commission of the Economic Community more strictly than in any other area except the United States.

The system of internationally affiliated collecting societies had been firmly established between the two World Wars, and under the rules prescribed by CISAC an elaborate system of accounting between societies had been set up. One of the basic principles was that no society could collect on the territory of another, and within almost all territories one society was an effective monopoly. No one could be a member of more than one society at the same time, and it was not a simple matter for a member to leave one society and join another[51].

Although perhaps one of the most perfect examples of effective international cooperation, the collecting societies realised that there was a growing movement against their monopoly powers by governments all over the world. They had been aware that the Commission was investigating the position of GEMA, the West German national society. (Gesellschaft fur musikische Auffuhrungs-und mechanische Vervielfaltigungsrechte.) On 3rd June 1970 the Commission decided to institute proceedings against that society. Its decision was given on 27th April 1971[52], and is known simply as re GEMA.

After setting out certain extracts from GEMA's constitution and statutes, the Commission drew attention to particular features contributing to its monopoly position, and showed how these offended against certain articles of the Treaty of Rome. GEMA is the only collecting society in West Germany operating in respect of musical performing rights, and corresponds to comparable societies in other Common

---

51 McFarlane, Copyright Collecting Societies, Grove's Dictionary of Music and Musicians, (6th edn.) (Macmillan).
52 [1971] C.M.L.R.D35.

Market countries. Only in Italy does a legal monopoly exist, where the collecting society, SIAE, is a quasi-government department, and its employees within the public sector[53].

Elsewhere in the member states, including West Germany, it would be possible for competing performing right societies to be established, so far as the law is concerned. This meant that in fact virtually every composer, author or publisher in Germany is obliged to join GEMA in order to exploit his rights - the same finding of fact as was made in most of the early cases involving PRS. The Commission also objected to the fact that a composer, author or publisher of a member state other than West Germany could never become a full voting member of GEMA, only an associate member, which placed him at a disadvantage economically. Not only does GEMA not operate directly outside its own territory, but also because of the system of reciprocity established between copyright collecting societies, a music user in Germany wishing to avail himself of non-German music still has to apply to GEMA for a licence.

By *Article 86, Treaty of Rome 1957*, it is incompatible with the Common Market for an undertaking to exploit in an improper manner a dominant position within the Common Market, or within a substantial part of it. The Commission found as a fact that GEMA is an undertaking within the meaning of Article 86, and having no competitor, it occupied a dominant position within West Germany, which itself constituted a substantial part of the Common Market. This dominant position it exploited in an improper manner, particularly as nationals of other member states cannot become full members of GEMA. It also abused its position in binding its members by obligations which were not object- ively justified, and which complicated the movement of its members from GEMA to another society. The Commission found it particularly offensive that GEMA demanded an assignment of copyright for all categories of works, and that moreover for the whole world. By its attitude GEMA showed that it wanted to turn its dominant position into an absolute monopoly. "GEMA", complained the Commission, "confused the necessity for collective management of performing rights with management by a single society which establishes and defends its exclusive position by improper means"[54].

This observation strikes at the whole root of copyright collecting societies in the form in which they are set up throughout the Western

---

53 McFarlane, Copyright Collecting Societies, Grove's Dictionary of Music and Musicians, (6th edn.) (Macmillan).
54 [1971] C.M.L.R.D35.

World, with the exception of the United States. Although in that country the main exercises of the performing right as described in this chapter is divided between ASCAP and BMI, there is no sign that elsewhere there are interests either willing or able to start up a particular society within a particular territory. Certainly in Western Europe, as exemplified by the Society in Britain, the existing monopoly societies have either consciously or unconsciously been able to build themselves into the fabric of the cultural life of the countries within which they operate. Scholarships are endowed, charities are fairly generously supported, and levies made from the earnings of currently successful members for distribution among other members and their dependents who may have fallen upon hard times[55]. Eminent personages are seen as guests of honour at PRS functions, and hard lobbying on the public relations front has bestowed some fair degree of respectability on the Society's operations. Although the BBC raised many arguments against the PRS demands during three long rate fixing hearings at arbitration and in front of the Performing Right Tribunal, at no time did it question the right of the Society to continue to function as it did, or suggest that the Corporation should set up a rival collecting society of its own, along the lines of the American Society BMI (Broadcast Music Inc.)

Indeed, during the Commission's investigation of GEMA, the organisation of chief music users, which might be supposed to be hostile, took up the cudgels on behalf of the copyright owners. In a letter from the European Broadcasting Union to the Commission it was said "If competition were to be artificially created in this sphere it would be to the detriment of broadcasting organisations which, far from deriving benefit from it, would suffer consequences economically harmful to them." It suggested that, on the contrary, the Commission "would be well advised to recommend to the governments concerned to insert provisions in their domestic legislations for the setting up of a jurisdictional, arbitration or ratifying body with powers . . . to determine the royalty payable by the broadcasting organisations to the society controlling the world-wide repertoire"[56].

The Commission, on the contrary, went even further in its criticism of GEMA's practices. Its members, said the Commission, should be free to decide whether they wished to assign to GEMA or to a foreign collecting society, all or any part of their rights for those countries in which GEMA did not carry on a direct activity. They should be free to decide whether they wished to assign entirely their rights for countries where GEMA

55 See "Performing Right", Spring 1965,p.18.
56 Letter of 4th June 1969. Cited in Wallace,"Control Over Copyright Monopolies",
   (1973) 4 IIC 382.

operates directly, or to divide them by categories among several authors' rights societies. Also, and probably most important in practical terms, a member should be free to decide whether he wished to withdraw from GEMA the administration of certain categories of rights after giving due notice, and without being subject to any penalty as a result of doing so. This however was not to prevent GEMA from demanding in West Germany where it carried on direct activity the exclusive assignment of all a writer's works, including future works.

Objection was also taken by the Commission to the classification of certain types of light music, and in connection with this, the operation of a social fund, in so far as GEMA by its constitution sought to exclude all claims of right by individual members, and any recourse by them to the courts. It has already been shown that the practice of the collecting societies, including, in the U.K., PRS, is to subsidise distribution to classical composers at the expense of popular composers, and to make deductions from collected revenues in respect of social funds, such as the PRS Members' Fund described above. These deductions are often weighted against the more successful composers.

Because of its dominant position GEMA was not entitled to exclude recourse to the courts, and it was no answer for the Society to claim that it was subjected to administrative supervision, for that did not guarantee to each member individually that his rights would be protected. The system of paying loyalty bonuses only to certain members was also objected to, as certain categories of members were excluded, and such payments would accordingly be made at their expense. It was this element of paying bonuses with funds fed from all the members to which the Commission objected, rather than the subsidy of classical music at the expense of successful light music.

Despite the formation of BMI (Broadcast Music Inc.) in the United States, music users in the form of broadcasting organisations have shown little inclination to take over authors' societies in Europe, or even to set up their own societies. But in recent years a more insidious threat to their independence has appeared. More and more in the last decade music publishing houses have been taken over, either by record manufacturers, or by conglomerates in which record production contributed significantly to the profit. Record producers use as a basic commodity the mechanical right, (the right to record), generally for a fixed rate geared to the retail price of the record, and in the U.K. they enjoy a compulsory licence, by virtue of *S. 8 Copyright Act 1956*. The rate of royalty is negotiated between the record producers on the one hand, through the International Federation of the Phonographic Industry (IFPI), and the international federation of mechanical right societies on the other, the Bureau International de l'Édition Méchanique (BIEM).

181

Moreover, many mechanical right and performing right societies are under the same umbrella, as in GEMA[57]. As publishing houses are of course substantial members of authors' societies, the taking over of publishers by record producers was to allow a Trojan Horse into the inner counsels of the authors' societies.

GEMA attempted to overcome this problem by providing in its articles that certain composers, authors and publishers could be denied the status of ordinary member, and that such status could be withdrawn if a member became economically dependent on a music user. Its arguments that these provisions prevented a vertical integration which would have a negative effect on the market from the composition point of view did not fall on entirely deaf ears within the Commission. It took the point that some degree of control of the position was desirable, but again having regard to GEMA's dominant position, considered that the refusal or withdrawal of membership went too far. It would suffice, the members of the Commission considered, if GEMA employed the least restrictive means; it would have been satisfied if GEMA had merely refused voting rights to the members in question when negotiation of contracts with music users was taking place, or required that the representative of a particular company should carry on a genuine publishing activity, and not at the same time be in the employ of a music user.

These views of the Commission seem a little naive. It is not inconceivable that within a particular territory, most if not all of the lending publishers could fall into the control of music users, thus placing half of the governing body of a particular society out of court in vital negotiations at which only the writers could represent the authors' society. Furthermore, few key employees of subsidary companies can be totally independent of their controlling shareholder on any issue which vitally affects the interests of that controlling company.

The Commission also took objection to the methods by which GEMA sought to prevent its members leaving, and moving to another collecting society. Among these was the requirement that the member should assign his rights to GEMA for a six year period. The Commissioners were not impressed by GEMA's plea that such a period was necessary to allow long term licences to be concluded with music users, as the assignment between GEMA and the members allowed the society to negotiate such agreements even after the member's assignment had ended. The assignment given by a new member also gave the society rights in future works not affected by termination of membership. This was felt to have

---

57 McFarlane, Copyright Collecting Societies, Grove's Dictionary of Music and Musicians, (6th edn.) (Macmillan).

no relevance to the negotiation of licences with music users, but was in reality merely an impediment to an author changing his collecting society.

Lastly, in so far as is relevant to this study, the Commission took exception to GEMA's restrictions limiting full membership in the case of publishers to those registered in West Germany, and relegating publishers which had not established at least a subsidiary in that territory to associate membership. This acted against the establishment of a single market in the supply of the services of a music publisher.

As a result of these findings, GEMA was ordered to alter its constitution, and to put an end to the practices complained of. The society immediately gave notice of appeal, which had the effect of staying execution of the decision, and as appeals take a long time to be formulated in this forum, GEMA had over a year to decide its final course of action. Consultation with its fellow members in CISAC was difficult, for GEMA had not gone out of its way to court friendship in recent years, and was suspected by many of its sister societies of wishing to squeeze them out of their territories, and so to establish a monopoly in Europe. At the time of the decision a number of other European societies took some pleasure in the discomfiture of GEMA.

There existed however a school of thought which felt that by adopting the recommendations of the Commission, GEMA or any other national society with expansive ambitions might more easily be able to spread its operations to territories other than its own, and to force small national societies, which had hitherto enjoyed a protected position within their own territory, out of business. It may be that something of this nature had occurred to the administrators of GEMA, for in 1972 they abandoned their appeal, and accepted the position. At the time of writing, the world of authors' societies is still in turmoil as a result of the Commission's decision, for not only have they failed to decide on a final common course of action, but they have as yet not obtained any clear guide as to what the ultimate practical effect of the implementation of the decision will be.

Undoubtedly the smaller societies fear very much for their future, which cannot really have been the intention of the draftsmen of Articles 85 and 86 of the Treaty of Rome. The controllers of PRS would not welcome the competition of the French or German national societies on U.K. territory, with perhaps a conflict between the societies as each tries to lure members from the others by offering more attractive terms. Certainly something of this kind has taken place as between ASCAP and BMI in America. The position of PRS in all this is rather ambiguous, for at times its administrators regard it as a large Continental society along the lines of SACEM in France or GEMA in West Germany, and at other

183

times they regard it as the natural leader of the smaller societies, and accordingly at risk from any expansion by the really larger societies.

William Wallace, late Assistant Comptroller General of the Patent Office in London, and one of the most respected voices in international copyright circles, has published an interesting analysis of the EEC Commission's review of GEMA[58]. He makes the eminently practical point that if the logical result of the decision were to be carried through, there might be a multiplicity of collecting societies, each controlling within Germany or any other member state of the Community, the rights of different groups of authors. This would be a very considerable impediment to a music user, who would have to attempt to look up lists in order to discover which collecting society controlled the rights in the particular work he wished to use, and whether he had that particular society's licence so to do. Indeed, it is extremely doubtful whether any current lists of titles to popular works which would be of any value could be prepared, taking into consideration the rapid changes in that area of the music world.

Wallace reaches the conclusion that anti-cartel laws are too blunt to be used for the control of this area of monopolies. Unlike most commentators he is neither a music user nor a copyright owner, and as he has spent most of his working life assessing the submissions of both sides, his view must be regarded as authoritative. There is, he says, a public interest in the fact of monopoly in this area, and other ways are available to control that monopoly. In Denmark for example the collecting society KODA is specifically exempted from the effect of the Danish anti-monopoly law[59]. Other ways are by the Canadian scheme of compulsory submission of copyright tariffs for approval in advance of their implementation, and the system of compulsory arbitration as is employed in the U.K. He recalls that before the Copyright Committee 1951, the Performing Right Society "very sensibly" raised no objection to the idea of compulsory arbitration over its tariffs.

He considers that the system of the Performing Right Tribunal in the U.K. appears to work very well on the whole, and that it is on occasion an advantage for Government to be able to point to the independence of the Tribunal in disclaiming responsibility for its decisions to dissatisfied music users "and on occasions the PRS itself"[60]. In my view he is entirely correct. There is nothing in the American experience or the

---

58 W. Wallace, "Control over the Monopoly Exercise of Copyright," 1973 IIC 380.
59 Monopolies and Restrictive Practices Act of 31st March, 1955 and June 4th 1965,s.2(2).
60 Supervision of Prices and Profits Act of April 2nd,1971,S.13(2).
   W. Wallace,op.cit.,p.386.

GEMA decision to demonstrate beyond doubt that the monopoly of the copyright societies is not in the public interest. Compulsory arbitration on any given rate provides an effective longstop, and there is a very real danger that if the monopoly were to be taken away, the international copyright system as it is known today would speedily collapse.

Professor Joliet is more critical of the GEMA decision still. He argues that without examining whether there are resultant abuses in the market which GEMA exploits, there is implicitly such abuse from the market-sharing arrangements evidenced by the terms of membership which might more properly have been considered under Article 85. Indeed, he calls into question whether it is in fact in the best interests of authors, composers and publishers to have the power to choose between a plurality of collecting societies[61].

---

61 Professor Rene Joliet, ''L'abuse de position dominante dans l'article 86 de Traité de Rome.'' 1973 Europarecht 17.

13

Possible Extension of Statutory Rights

Whenever the performing right was threatened during the course of its fight for recognition and establishment, what was in reality at stake was an economic right. This was true whether the threat lay in private actions in the courts to dispute the liability of the music user to pay for that utilisation, or whether it came from governmental or supra-governmental operations enquiring into monopolistic aspects of copyright exploitation. Although in theory the performing right can be employed to prevent people using a work against the wishes of the copyright owner, ownership is now almost entirely exercised as a means of obtaining compensation for the use or performance of a composition in which the rights are held by a particular individual or corporation.

The right is entirely statutory, copyright in published works being held no longer to exist at common law since the *Statute of Anne (8 Anne c.19)* by the case of *Donaldson v. Beckett*[1,2]. Therefore until the *Dramatic Copyright Act 1833* there was no performing right in the U.K. in respect of which a copyright owner could obtain payment in respect of the use of his work by its performance.

It is tempting to suggest that the reason why the introduction of a performing right was so long delayed in the first place lay in an absence of commercial initiative in the more prosperous sections of the community, and that the subsequently serious exploitation of the right in Britain was put off for the best part of a century because of our innate conservatism and hostility to new ideas[3]. But this is very probably wide of the mark, and other reasons must be sought for the inactivity. The argument is certainly not consistent with the deliberate practice of the sheet music publishers in the nineteenth century in offering their wares free of performing rights.

---

1 (1774) 4 Burr.2408.
2 It probably continues to exist in respect of unpublished literary dramatic and musical works. See **S.2 (3)Copyright Act 1956** and the contradiction in Copyright (Copinger & Skone-James) (11th edn.para.5)
3 It is currently fashionable to account for the British economic malaise along these lines. See e.g. Corelli Barnett, ''What's wrong with Britain'',Sunday Telegraph, 26th January 1975.

Nevertheless there is no divine right of copyright in the United Kingdom which somehow exists outside the legal system, as French writers sometimes claim exists in Continental jurisdictions. Thus; "En empruntant les élèments d'un dispositif de protection des droits voisin au régime des oeuvres de l'esprit, les législateurs des pays d'inspiration latine ont recours à une fiction comparable à celle dont se servait le prêteur romain lorsqu'il se trouvait devant une situation jurideque qui aurait dû etre protégée par le droit civil mais qui, faute d'une condition juridique, ne pouvait bénéficier de cette protection. De même que le prêteur procédait à une extension du droit civil pour des raisons d'utilité évidente, de même le législateur moderne opère un transfert arbitraire des droits d'auteur pour protéger les prestations des auxiliaries de la création artistique ou littéraire"[4].

The performing right in this country is a piece of property, albeit intangible, which depends for its existence on a statute, just as all the other rights existing by virtue of the *Copyright Act 1956*. Until the passage of a statute granting the performing right, there was no right, and if the *Copyright Act 1956* were now to be repealed, there would be no performing right, until some new statute granting it were passed. Its initial enactment was eventually secured because sufficient pressure was brought to bear by parties having an interest in the matter. But it is always upon pressure that the passage of these rights ultimately depends; there is really no "natural justice" as their adherents sometimes claim. It is only Parliamentary muscle.

For example, if the performing artistes had been sufficiently well organised at the right time, they might have obtained a right of property in their performances recorded on film or record, but by the time that their representatives were alive to the possibility, the composers, or more accurately the interests behind them, made great efforts to ensure that new economic benefits from royalties derived from performing rights should not be extended to them. The conflict has generally taken place in areas not the subject of this work, at international conferences where the performers' and authors' organisations have clashed[5]. But clearly there are over-lapping areas, and the performers have a case. Some performances contain an element of composition in the form of improvisation. Some performers are in such a strong contractual position that they can insist on royalties in respect of repeats of their filmed or recorded performances, which in effect amount to performing rights.

---

4 Dock. Étude sur le Droit d'Auteur, p.167.
5 See McFarlane, "The Rome Convention 1961", LLM thesis in the University of Sheffield.

But still the rights of the performer in law in the U.K. are only criminal, and likely to remain so.

It can be argued that if the statutory performing right in this country were to be for some reason repealed, the gap would be filled by the common law, that is to say that judges faced with an absence of a statutory performing right would return to the old common law principles which existed prior to the *Statute of Anne 1709.* But this is scarcely convincing. A copyright law of sorts exists in practically every state in the world at the present time, and in every case the vehicle is a statute. It is not a practical proposition to operate the sophisticated rights involved in this form of protection without clearly specifying in a code the extent of the right and the protection provided.

The concept of statutory rights may be used to open up fresh fields of income for such creative producers or their commercial exploiters as can obtain the passage of enabling legislation. Pressure for a public lending right for literary authors and their publishers has been gradually building up over the last twenty years or more; perhaps because of the increasing merger of literary and music publishing interests in the same conglomerate in recent years that pressure has recently come to a head. So forceful has been the campaign by the proponents of the new right, through Parliament and the press, that organised opposition from library interests and local authorities has latterly been subdued. The addition of music publishing interests to the campaign doubtlessly added considerable expertise to the lobbying.

The author of the present work has outlined the early history of lobbying in this country for the right[6]. As long ago as 1951 a campaign was begun by the novelist John Brophy to levy an old penny from the borrower on each occasion that a book was borrowed from a public library. This was intensified when the Roberts Committee was set up in 1957 to investigate the library system, but it made no reference to the subject of compensation for authors in respect of library borrowing in its report, and in the event the "Brophy Penny" was never levied. Subsequent attempts to introduce a public lending right by Bills failed in 1960, 1961 and 1964, but they served in drawing attention to the demands of authors, and gradually the campaign increased. A later proposal was that compensation should be based on the stocks of copyright books held by libraries, but librarians were opposed to the additional work involved, and this suggestion also foundered. The Society of Authors accordingly devised an amended scheme whereby

---

6 McFarlane,"Public Lending Rights", 1971 JBL 34.

details of titles sold to libraries by the publishers could be recorded by wholesalers, and by 1971 there was general expectation in the literary world that the introduction of the new right was imminent.

The Conservative Government after taking office in 1970 had on several occasions appeared to support the right, without specifying what form it would take when it was introduced. But as time went by it seemed less and less likely that the Government intended to introduce the necessary legislation itself, but that it would be left to a private member to do so. The problem was clearly one of "Who is to pay for the new right?". Speaking at a Press Club dinner the then Minister for the Arts, Norman St.John-Stevas, said, "Where was the money to be found to compensate authors for the lending of their books, and how could a scheme be devised which would be simple to operate and not consume in administration such money as we may be able to find? One thing I can make quite clear; the Government does not believe it would be right to seek to recoup the cost by direct charge on members of the public using the library service. Library charges are not a starter"[7].

In the autumn of 1973, Ernle Money, then Conservative member for Ipswich, who had drawn fourth place in the private members' ballot, introduced his Public Lending Right Bill. This embodied the apparently simple solution of adding to the rights restricted by copyright in *Sections 2 & 3 Copyright Act 1956* the right of "lending the work to the public". By February 1974, despite the observations of Mr. St.John-Stevas, the Bill seemed well on its way to a third reading when Parliament was dissolved, the Conservative administration defeated at the polls, and the Bill lapsed.

But it is doubtful if its sponsors fully appreciated the implications of their drafting if the Bill had then passed into law. The right to lend would initially have been vested in the first owner of the copyright, who could have assigned it to any collecting society which might have been established, but he could also have insisted on licensing it direct if he had so chosen. More crucial still is that an author would have been entitled additionally to refuse to lend his work, so that a new power would have been granted to literary men who for one reason or another objected to their works being on the shelves of public libraries. Presumably in such an event the Performing Right Tribunal would not have been able to interfere, as it can only deal with licensing bodies operating scemes, and not with individuals licensing their works on their own account.

"Mr. Heath's government, just as the succeeding Labour administration, judged the scheme to be a particularly prickly plant." To quote

---

7 Daily Telegraph,24th January 1974.

Norman St.John-Stevas again, "This is one of the most intricate problems I have come across"[8]. Despite the rallying cry employed at the time of 'Justice for Authors', it is clear that if the right had been introduced in the form envisaged by Mr. Money's Bill, publishers would have stood to gain a considerable windfall. And what would have been the position with foreign authors whose works are stocked in British libraries? Was it intended that they would receive payment, or perhaps only those whose governments were prepared to offer reciprocity to British authors?"

But the greatest problem of all was that of the manner of payment. The effect of Ernle Money's Bill would have been that the user of the right footed the account, but both Labour and Conservative administrations indicated that they will not tolerate a charge to the user, for "tax on knowledge" is a subject which has always aroused strong emotions in Britain. There were some indications that it was to be met by a charge on local authority rates, but this was vetoed by central government.

In 1974 the Society of Authors produced an estimate that a minimum of £4,000,000 per annum would be required to operate a public lending right system[9]. As there are at present about 3,500 members of the Society of Authors, this would produce income per member of over £1,000. In their campaign for the right, the authors' representatives have made great play of the statistic that only about one author in six earns more than about £1,000 per annum from his writing[10]. It may therefore be that their expectations have been raised too high. PRS, it will be recalled, did not make any distribution to its members until 1917, three years after it began trading[11].

Renewed efforts were made to introduce a private members' Bill on the subject after the victory of the Labour Party in the second General Election of 1974. Those concerned were dissuaded by Governmental undertakings that a Bill would be brought in at an early date, but by Easter 1975, Hugh Jenkins, then Minister for the Arts, told authors' representatives that the Bill was to be put back to the autumn for further discussion of how the cost of the right was to be met.

Without a law, there is no right. With a law, there is immediately a right. If Edward Heath had not been defeated in February 1974, and

---

8 Daily Telegraph,24th January 1974.
9 Daily Telegraph,24th January 1974.
10 McFarlane,"Public Lending Rights", 1971 JBL 37, citing Victor Bonham Carter of the Society of Authors.
11 See Chapter 6 ante.

Ernle Money's Bill had passed on the third reading, it would have become law as such, without any qualifications as to how it was to be paid for. Although the Government may not have wanted it thus, it would not have been able to stop it had there been a majority for the measure in the House on a Private Member's Bill; it is highly unlikely that the Government would at that time have put the whips on to defeat it.

When Mr. Money's Bill lapsed, it was followed in 1976 by yet another proposal, similar in form and design to the one which has now passed into law. However a small but determined band of members of Parliament again put up fierce opposition to it, and it was abandoned by the Government before it finished its report stage. Supporters of the measure could have been forgiven for feeling despondent by this time; for over fifteen years one defeat had succeeded another, and the prospect of eventual victory appeared further away than ever.

It was thus a considerable surprise to many when a fresh Bill was brought in during the last session of Mr. Callaghan's administration to which opposition was limited, and its progress in consequence swift. It did not contain some of the more controversial proposals which had held back earlier Bills, and enjoying a clear run, it passed its third reading shortly prior to the dissolution of Parliament, receiving the Royal Assent on 22 March, to be known as the Public Lending Right Act 1979.

Consisting of five sections and a schedule, it enshrines the principle that Public Lending Right is a grant to authors of an entitlement to receive payments from a central fund in respect of their books lent to the public by particular local authorities in the United Kingdom. But PLR is not a right in the nature of copyright, which is essentially an unfettered right vested in the copyright owner to do certain acts in respect of a copyright work, or to prevent others from doing those acts without his permission. The economic significance of copyright lies in the entitlement to exploit this protection for gain.

But the Public Lending Right Act 1979 accords no such right to authors. Although described by the draftsman as a right, what authors have acquired is an entitlement to share in the division of a fund set up by the state, where control of the amount of money available for distribution is also vested in the state. This money is not a royalty earned in respect of the use of the work by a licensed user, but derives from the author having obtained a share of a subsidy or grant upon which an upper limit is set. The implications of these limitations for the whole copyright system are slightly dangerous in an age of state intervention; its supporters will hope that the introduction of public lending right in its present form is merely a prelude to subsequent expansion into a right akin to copyright as established in the Copyright Act 1956. It would be

192

unfortunate if the reverse were to take place, and true copyright became replaced by state subsidies; if this suggestion were ever put forward today, immediate and fierce opposition from the literary, musical and artistic sections of the community would be inevitable. But having been introduced in this form in the United Kingdom, it seems more likely to expand when the economy recovers, and as similar rights are introduced in other countries, it could eventually be incorporated into the Berne and Universal Copyright Conventions.

The Public Lending Right Act sets up a framework for the so-called right, but a good deal is left to be filled in later through a scheme provided for in the statute. By this scheme are to be determined classes, descriptions and categories of books in respect of which the right exists, and the scheme is also to establish the scale of payments. The Secretary of State is to consult interested parties, who include the representatives of authors and library authorities, so although in statute form, there is still much to be worked out inside the broad limits of the Act.

A registrar is to be appointed to administer the scheme, who is to be responsible for maintaining a register of works and their authors. Where the right is transmitted to another person under the scheme, the registrar is to record the person for the time being entitled to the right. He is to appoint a staff, and an early estimate is that his office will require the employment of about 35-40 additional staff.

The central fund is to be financed by money provided by Parliament, which is not to exceed £2 million a year, although the power exists to increase this by order subject to resolution of the House of Commons. But when account is taken of the fact that from this £2 million are to be met all the expenses of administering the scheme, quite apart from the cost of the salaries of the registrar and his staff, it is evident that at least in the early years, there is not going to be a great deal available for division between the entitled authors. However the principle of the Public Lending Right has been established, and that reflects a great deal of credit on those representatives of authors' rights who have fought so hard for its introduction over so many years.

Other states have granted different rights in the form of monopolies which are rather less likely to be introduced in Britain. There is for example the paying public domain[12], whereby the post-mortem period of copyright protection is extended for a further period, and the funds accrue to the state, generally for the support of the arts. There is also the *droit de suite*, which is not a monopoly, but which nonetheless depends on a statute. It accords to the artist a right to a percentage of the

---

12 See Henry Cecil, The Times, 11th February 1974.

increased value on subsequent sales of their works of plastic art[13]. The state considers in these cases that the artist should share in the fruits of any multiplication in the value of his work due to belated recognition of his talent.

It was the determination and advocacy of Bulwer Lytton which eventually pushed the *Dramatic Copyright Act 1833* through Parliament, but this was followed by the inactivity of the music publishers who failed to grasp the economic significance of the performing right when it was extended to musical works by the *Literary Copyright Act 1842*. The belated foundation of the Performing Right Society soon demonstrated to the entertainment world that a major source of income could be derived from the right, and eventually the gramophone interests were alerted to the possibilities. The arguments put forward on their behalf in *Gramophone Company Ltd. v. Carwardine*[14] have a fairly devious appearance when contrasted with the submissions made to the architects of the *Copyright Act 1911*, and the Copyright Committee of 1951 was not slow to point this out. But despite this, the gramophone lobby was strong enough at the time to ensure that their right was enclosed in *S.12 Copyright Act 1956*, so that, once there, the argument as to liability was at end.

Undoubtedly new technical developments will call for further protection within the copyright or related systems, and the copyright system is for this purpose more flexible than the patent system. The key to the matter is, first, agreement that the need for a particular right exists, second, the enactment of the right, and third, the machinery to administer that right effectively. The development of the performing right in Britain is the reflection of a system in respect of which each of these conditions has been satisfied.

---

13   McFarlane,"Artists and the Droit de Suite."Law Guardian, September 1970,p.43.
14   [1934]Ch.450.

Table of Cases

Table of Statutes and Conventions

INDEX

Table of Cases

Table of Statutes and Conventions

199

INDEX

200

203